Working Free

Working Free

Practical Alternatives to the 9 to 5 Job

JOHN APPLEGATH

amacom

A division of American Management Associations

Library of Congress Cataloging in Publication Data

Applegath, John.
   Working free.

   Includes index.
    1. Work 2. Hours of labor. 3. Occupations.
I. Title.
HD4905.A64   331.25'72   81-69373
ISBN 0-8144-5658-8   AACR2
ISBN 0-8144-7582-5 pbk

Third Printing

For Molly,
with the hope that she will find joy in her work.

I would like to thank the Ford Foundation for its grant in support of my work on this book. Thanks go also to Avon Mattison, who conducted several of the interviews.

Foreword

What's alternative today is mainstream tomorrow.

In the twenty-first century, technological advances will put a rising floor of material comfort under every American, and the innovators will have no more success in hogging the gains for themselves than they did in the past. The growing end of today's economy is in human work that can't be done by reluctant clockwatchers. The jobless prosperity ahead will redistribute the work that remains by age and sex and change not only the nature of work but the way we feel about it.

Working Free is a progress report on this future. Today more people are working what John Applegath so felicitously calls "less than full time." More people are working off the books. More people are working at home. There is greater emphasis on psychic rather than dollar pay, which means that you can't get the garbagemen to come up your hill at any price, while more people are opting for the volunteer work no one will pay for. Much of the work of the future is being invented because people like to do it.

The alternatives will become the mainstream for the simple and sufficient reason that everyone wants it. Work rules have always been limited by what you can get the workers to do. *Working Free* shows us how enterprising workers are wiggling out of the straitjacket of jobs that misinterpret their motives. It can be read as a guide to the way you can work around the rules, get out of a job that frustrates you, restructure your job into freelance work, and learn to control your tasks and your schedule.

Women have been the vanguard. Mothers found ways to stay on the job by trading off lunch hour for coming in an hour later in the morning. Women went back to school after their children were grown and started a new career that utilized skills they had learned in rearing a family.

While women were leading the way, men envied the balance they were striking between work and the rest of their lives. Some men began to realize that they were tired of the old nine-to-five routine and were ready for a midlife change of career themselves. Relieved of sole responsibility for the bills, husbands too began to think of ways to trade money for leisure or better control over their working lives.

The biggest impact of the two-paycheck marriage will ultimately prove to be on the motivations of men. What employers call the decline of the old work ethic is the decline in the number of breadwinning fathers who will "do anything" for the sake of his wife and kids at home. The employers who thrive will be those who invent incentives that engage these supposedly "alternative" workers.

Old people are pioneers. A majority say they want to retire early, but in the same breath they can be made to say that they want to go on working. What they really mean is that they want to retire from their lockstep, deadend jobs and do part-time work or work they like better. Many of them are using a modest retirement income to help in the exciting task of inventing the future.

Applegath's future sounds visionary, but it is straight up the track of our long historical perspective. What is that future? Rewarding rather than demeaning work. A higher income floor. Improvements in the quality of worklife through the relinquishment of classic management prerogatives. Insistence on psychic as well as money pay. The professionalization of uneconomic work that volunteers do because it is badly needed. Finally, the technology ahead may well receive the doctrines of Adam Smith by encouraging a renaissance of small free enterprisers who will risk their personal savings to do the work they want to do.

Caroline Bird

Contents

1 Introduction 1
2 Alternatives to the 9 to 5 Routine 12
3 Why People Leave Traditional Jobs 22
4 Values, Attitudes, Priorities, and Motivation 40
5 Risks and Problems 52
6 The Rewards 62
7 Money 72
8 Managing Time 88
9 Work and the Rest of Your Life 102
10 Working at Home 117
11 Security—The Future 126
12 Getting Your Act Together 135
13 Support Systems and Networks 151
14 Some Enlightened Employers 161
15 A Modest Proposal for a Rational System of
   Allocating Work 171
16 A Scenario for Work in the Future 178
Research and Resource Information 192
Index 203

1

Introduction

Affecting any discussion of the work ethic is the terrible ambiguity of the word "work" itself. . . . Work is the tedious routine of the assembly line and the . . . toil of those who collect the trash. . . . It is also the wonderfully self-rewarding occupation of the musician, painter, surgeon, lawyer, engineer, scientist, or business executive. Work is what members of Congress and the President of the United States spend millions of dollars to be allowed to do. It is ridiculous that one word should be used to cover such diverse conditions.

> —John Kenneth Galbraith
> The Work Ethic: It Works Best
> for Those Who Work Least,
> *The Progressive,* June 1981.

Terry Mollner works two hours a day, five days a week. His average annual income is around $16,000.

Mike Galbraith is a cook in a Toronto restaurant from November through April. During the summer he's the chef and his wife, Jane, is the dining-room hostess at a summer resort on a Canadian lake. In a typical recent year they spent the month of May traveling and visiting friends in New England and the month of October sailing and enjoying the laid-back life in California.

For several years, Sam Love was able to earn all the money he needed by working three months of the year—the rest of his time was devoted to something else he felt he needed more than money: time to think and do a little writing.

Pat Lee has worked for many different employers, including a fair number of free-lance and temporary jobs. With a few exceptions, they would all love to have her on the payroll now. But a few years ago Pat decided she would work only when and where she wanted to, and she has turned her varied work experience into a lucrative career as a consultant and special-projects manager for employers of her choosing.

Jay Levinson currently earns money in at least seven different ways—none of which is his career. He doesn't have a career—doesn't believe in them.

Suzanne Baer is Director of Career Counseling at Marymount Manhattan College. So is Joan Likely Cosenza. Suzanne works about half of each week and Joan the other half—at the same job.

Mike Marien is the editor of *Future Survey,* a major monthly reference publication of the World Future Society, and works from 9 to 5, five or six days a week. The World Future Society is located in Washington, D.C. Mike works in a cozy office in his old farmhouse in a beautiful rural area of upstate New York. He works from 9 to 5—except for occasional time out for a stroll, or to do a little weeding in the garden—because he *chooses* to. He has found that this is the way he is most productive.

Don Metzger works almost literally around the clock for much of the year, earning a very good salary as a pilot on the St. Lawrence Seaway. From December to April, Don and his wife are usually scuba diving in the Caribbean.

Wendy Burns and Robin Graves, both mothers of very young children, felt a desperate need for some creative activity as a relief from the diaper scene. One day they got together over Wendy's kitchen table and started designing and making simple, attractive canvas bags. Now they find themselves running a business that employs several other women from time to time who all work at home.

In the pages that follow, you will learn more about Terry and Pat and Jay and Don and a number of other highly productive people who have discovered that it is possible to work on one's own terms and to suit one's own preferences, instead of punching a clock from 9 to 5. Should you decide to read further, I hope that you may also come to see through and beyond the current "common sense" view of such things as "the work ethic," "productivity," "standard of living," "incentive," "compensation," "security," "advancement," "creativity." Finally, I hope it becomes clear that the traditional "military" model by which most work is organized survives only as long as individuals choose to put up with it.

This is not to suggest that there is anything inherently bad about showing up at the office or plant and fitting into someone else's routines from 8:30 to 4:30, five days a week. Many, many people thrive on that kind of rhythm and on order imposed by somebody else. I am genuinely happy for them. I feel less good about the thousands—perhaps hundreds of thousands—whose productivity, creativity, and enjoyment of life are apparently severely stifled by the rigidity of the standard factory or office-work routines.

And since writing is always partly self-confession, let me admit that my personal bias reflects the nonroutine, nonconventional position. Having lived for 46 years, having worked for money for 30 of them, and having paid a lot of attention to what was going on, I am absolutely certain that I have been *least* productive and creative during the times when someone else told me when and where to show up and how to do things. I will say that my particular brand of productivity and creativity has not made me rich—indeed, poverty is not unfamiliar to me, although it is by no means a condition I would choose. And I have had the good fortune during most of the time I worked for someone else's organization to have had immediate superiors who wanted my creations and products more than they wanted to see my face in a fixed location during preset hours.

There are different kinds of people, with different kinds of personal values and priorities, different biological rhythms, different work habits. Most of the formal literature on work, whether published in the business press, in sociological journals, or in government reports, appears not to recognize these variations. It is my hope that this book will help a bit to change that picture and to clarify for all of us the nature of reality in the world of work.

Some of us, whose best work sometimes gets done at 4:00 A.M., or in the company of special friends, or on the deck of a sailboat, are tired of being viewed as odd. We also think IBM and Imperial Oil and the Ford Motor Company could learn some useful things from our experiences. If nothing else, after reading this book you are likely to become aware of more of us in your environment than you had ever realized. In fact, among my own friends at least half have unconventional work arrangements. Of course we do choose our companions—except, that is, in the case of a friend who recently complained about the backbiting colleagues she had to spend her day with. She's thinking of making a change. . . .

In the United States, the public's perception of work and workers suffers from considerable distortion and serious limitations. When you think of "the workers," what picture comes to mind? People doing data processing? A salesperson making calls? A transcontinental truck driver?

People in the shipping room of a small high-technology manufacturing business? Secretaries and file clerks?

It is a reasonable bet that your immediate image of "workers" was none of these, and a very high probability that it was a picture of people in a factory assembly line—in a *large* factory with a *lot* of noise and dirt.

But, in fact, not more than 20 percent of our workforce is engaged directly in manufacturing.* This means that 80 percent are doing something else—waiting on customers in stores and restaurants, washing cars, selling magazine subscriptions over the telephone or insurance policies in offices and living rooms, teaching night-school classes in accounting or auto mechanics, driving delivery trucks, preparing food in restaurants or in dormitories or in private clubs, cutting hair, running errands for television producers, writing newspaper articles, mowing hay, driving ambulances, pounding police beats, sorting or delivering mail, and several thousand other things.

Another prevalent view of work that is rapidly becoming obsolete holds that if you are not working according to someone else's schedule, at someone else's convenience or locations, you're not really *working*. We must begin to broaden our concept of the world of work if we are going to properly understand the range of opportunities for earning a living that actually exists.

Over the years, thousands of studies and millions of pages have been written on the subject of work. The vast majority of the formal analyses have described people in traditional workplaces—factories and offices, usually in large organizations—and have shown an extreme imbalance toward that 20 percent of the working population employed in factories. For this reason, the idea of "the

*The RAND Corporation estimates that within 20 years this figure will be only 2 percent.

world of work" operating in the social sciences and much
of the public consciousness is one of assembly-line factory
workers who appear at their place of work each day, five
days a week, at 8:00 or 9:00 A.M., perform endless routine
tasks, and leave for home around 4:00 or 5:00 P.M.

It has often been noted that the organization of our
formal system of education—the public schools—came to
consciously emulate this factory work model of rigid time
and place constraints and standard routines. The model
has been so pervasive in so many areas that even our arrangements for treating illness have evolved into giant factories called hospitals where technology and time
schedules rule the day and traditional notions of healing
seem out of place.

These days most people work in some kind of office,
usually handling some sort of information. The processing
of information can be handled in many different ways.
Probably the only reason so many offices are run like factories lies in the fact that with only a few exceptions, such
as banks and insurance companies and newspapers, offices
were originally just a small portion of a factory.

It is interesting to speculate how the work of handling
information might have been organized if office managers
had not been so strongly programmed by the factory system and the school system, which resembles it. Had the
telephone been perfected before the factory, it might
never have occurred to anyone to travel to an office to
make telephone calls all day, as so many people now do.
And now that automated word-processing systems and
computers with remote terminals are the preferred ways
of handling information, it makes even less sense for people to leave their homes to edit manuscripts, write reports,
or process numbers. The vision of the near future for
many forward-looking people definitely includes what Alvin Toffler calls "the electronic cottage."

The fact is that the mode of work, of "earning a living"—for many people and for increasing numbers in recent years—has nothing to do with the factory model. The honorable and time-honored occupation of salesperson has always been characterized by an emphasis on getting results, making the sale, rather than on being at some particular place for some fixed number of hours each day or week. Schoolteachers have usually had three months of free time each year in which to do whatever they pleased. And thousands of college professors have not only that free time to use as they wish, but aside from faculty meetings and a few hours a week when they must appear in classrooms, they are largely free to come and go as they please—and *going* may just as well include numerous trips around the country to attend conferences or to do consulting to earn extra money, or a year's paid sabbatical that may be spent in Ireland or Tanzania. A far cry from 9 to 5.

Many people seem to *resent* the freedom and flexibility of the life of a college professor or a salesperson. At one time I was working for a company as a salesman, which meant that in order to accomplish anything I had to organize my own work and be on the road most of the time. And yet there were people in that organization who were convinced that the only time I was contributing to the company was when I was clearly visible at my desk in my office. No doubt some readers of this book have experienced the same attitude. Isn't this really a matter of people who have chosen to be ruled by routines and rigid structures imposing their values on the rest of us?

One of my motivations for writing this book is to show that *many people are most productive when their work arrangement provides maximum autonomy and flexibility.* It also seems important to me just to make unconventional work arrangements more visible to everyone. Many people are convinced that routine, rigidly structured work is the only possibility for them simply because they are unaware of alternatives.

In the pages that follow, we will learn about the work styles of a broad range of men and women in many different fields. People in widely different circumstances: single people with no financial responsibility for others as well as married heads of households with children to put through college; both young people and people over 70 who are still enjoying the process of creating or producing something for income; people who live quite comfortably on $5,000 or $6,000 a year, others who feel they must earn at least $25,000 but can't really enjoy life on less than $50,000, and people who earn $100,000 a year or more—all without a 9 to 5 job.

Important—this is not a book about "dropouts." It is also not a book about the other extreme—people who embark on such large-scale ventures as founding a substantial new business firm.

While interviewing for this book and discussing it with various people, one of the frequent comments I heard was some version of, "My job is an alternative to 9 to 5. I work from 7:00 A.M. till 10:00 P.M. most days." This is of course one of the choices people have, but we won't go into that one in this book because Marilyn Machlowitz has already written a very insightful book about workaholics.*

The example is not irrelevant, however, because the main message of this book is that *most of us do have some choices about how we will organize and manage that part of our lives which is devoted to earning income.* We can choose to make it the most important part of our lives to the point of becoming obsessed with our work; or we can choose to work only when we really need to accumulate some money and live very frugally the rest of the time (unless we have

*See Marilyn Machlowitz, *Workaholics*, Reading, Mass.: Addison-Wesley, 1980.

made a bundle in a few months or years and can afford to live in splendor for awhile without working). Most people end up choosing something in between, and many thoughtful people try to achieve some balance in their lives. That word balance emerged repeatedly in the interviews. It is clearly a crucial key for employers and policy-makers who wish to understand and deal creatively with the new work attitudes described in Chapter 3.

It is important to clarify some of the limits of this book. I have dealt essentially with people who would consider themselves "middle class." I have not included examples of people living and working in ghettos, although I would like to believe that some of the models and messages in this book could be applied to the problems of the poor and the unemployed.

I have also tried to avoid descriptions of people with inherited wealth, even though many of them, enjoying the financial freedom to do so, have devised quite interesting unconventional ways to be creative and productive. The point is that no matter how ingenious the devices these people have used to avoid the 9 to 5 routine, the rest of us will not be able to identify with them. Most of us really have to be concerned at all times with supporting ourselves and those dependent on us. All the people I have included here share this need.

With a few exceptions the people interviewed are all citizens of the United States and Canada. I have deliber-ately included a significant number of Canadians in order to redress a ridiculous imbalance in reports dealing with social phenomena in North America. Anyone who has spent time in Canada knows that the people who live in that country are not, by and large, different from U.S. citizens in any major way. Thousands of books have been written that give disproportionate weight to the experi-ences of people in New York City or California. We can gain just as much enlightenment from the experiences of people in Toronto, Ottawa, or Alcove, Quebec, as from those in Chicago or a Vermont village.

As long as I am describing the limits of this book, let me emphasize that I have not intended it to be a work of academic social science. Although an interview method has provided the basis for the information conveyed, I have deliberately avoided any attempt to present it as a formal survey research project. The purpose of the book is to give ordinary people a fresh perspective on work and some information, not to satisfy academic peers with impressive manipulations of statistics. I am less interested, as I think most people are, in the specific numbers or percentages of people in the workforce in any given year who happen to be employed on the basis of something other than 9 to 5, than in learning how these people manage their lives and work styles. I would like to think that this book will be just as useful to people ten years after publication as on the day it first appears. Current statistics about the workforce will be relatively meaningless in a very short time. Readers who feel the need for statistical reassurance that they will have lots of company if they become free-lancers or part-timers have only to turn to the latest statistics produced by the 9 to 5ers at the U.S. Department of Labor or the Labor Ministry of Canada. It's all there. No need to repeat it here.

Having said this, I feel impelled to add a note of particular appreciation to Robert Schrank and to the Ford Foundation for recognizing that important and useful information about social change can be generated and conveyed by people outside of academia. It is always safer for foundations to give money to highly credentialed individuals who are part of academic institutions. It is a genuine risk to support relatively unknown, independent creative persons. I hope that the result of my use of some of the Ford

Foundation's money will not prove an embarrassment to the good people there. On the other hand, nothing would please me more than to learn someday that the publication of this book helped initiate a more adventurous policy among foundations of giving grants to independent thinkers and others who do their best work unfettered by institutions.

One final point about what this book is not. In July 1980 I presented a workshop at the First World Congress of The World Future Society on the subject "Inventing Your Own Job." At the end of the session, I asked all those in attendance to write down something about what they got out of the workshop. I was delighted with the array of positive, even joyful responses—except for one. That person wrote, "This workshop gave me useful information about how to find a job." I couldn't believe it. Apparently, some people can be confronted with an intensive presentation that deals with something unconventional and can be so totally programmed toward the conventional that they miss the point entirely.

In case any of the readers of this book are in that category, let me announce once and for all: *This book is not about how to get a job*—at least not a traditional job. It is about designing the part of your life devoted to earning a living so that you can maximize your creativity, productivity, and enjoyment during every hour and every day of your life.

2

Alternatives to the 9 to 5 Routine

Different strokes for different folks.
—Anonymous

People living in democratic societies usually place high value on some concept of equality. But problems arise when we depart from the essential idea that all people should have equal access to opportunities in society and generalize that all human beings are, in fact, equal. We cause ourselves much unnecessary grief when we take another step and transform human "equality" into an extreme, inappropriate view that "everyone is pretty much alike." Granted, such homogenization of human beings is common in some parts of the world and in too many large bureaucracies right here at home (both corporate and governmental). And the work does get done. Nonetheless, in such circumstances, very few people are doing anything near the best they are capable of.

The fact is that the human race comprises a collection of persons of infinite variety and dimensions, and the more we are forced into standard molds, the less motivated we feel to reach our potential. Human variability is well documented. For example, Donald Fiske, a psychologist at the University of Chicago, has done a lot of careful research on such things as the differences in people's body clocks and other factors that may cause a person to perform better at one time of the day, or month, or week than at another.* His work suggests that a wide range of needs and habits among individuals should be considered "normal."

Nonetheless, most work in industralized countries is organized to fit the preferences of early risers and compulsively routinized types. As one might expect, a whole lot of people who are uncomfortable in these rigid structures and fixed routines are made to feel that there must be something wrong with them. Often these are very creative people. Organizations that cannot accommodate, let alone encourage, so-called divergent personalities may be missing out on valuable contributions from people whose best work gets done at 11:00 P.M., or people who tend to "fall apart" on Mondays or on Fridays, or when the moon is full.

So what happens? Two things: (1) most people adapt to somebody else's preferred routines, thereby compromising their own potential productivity; and (2) others—the risk takers—find or *invent* some way to earn a living that allows them to work when they are most productive.

It is not solely a matter of personality differences, however, that motivate some people to seek alternative work arrangements. Modern lives in industrial societies are extremely complex. People have other things to do besides earning a living. Child care is an obvious one. And in the transition we are experiencing from an industrial econ-

*See Donald W. Fiske, "The Constraint on Intra-Individual Variables in Test Responses," *Education and Psychological Measurement 17,* 1957, 317–331; see also Jane E. Brody, "Body's Rhythms Send Messages on When to Work and When to Play," *The New York Times,* Aug. 11, 1981. This is a survey of recent work at several major medical research centers.

omy to a "service and information" economy, many people are finding that it is necessary to have some time off to learn something new at various times in the life cycle. This new need for continuing formal learning requires more free time on a regular basis. One round of "education" early in one's life is no longer sufficient.

Some people just function better over the long range with time off occasionally for whatever leisure activities will reinvigorate them. Jay Levinson, one of the people interviewed for this book, spoke at length about how important it was for him and his wife to go off backpacking for a few days once or twice a month.

According to the traditional work ethic, this kind of work style might seem to suggest irresponsible behavior. But as we shall see, many of the people who have taken the trouble to find or create unconventional work arrangements are often much more productive and efficient than people bound to traditional office time clocks and regimented work lives. Because many of them in fact "work" fewer hours does not mean that they produce less. And if producing is evaluated in terms of *quality* as well as quantity, many large, bureaucratic corporations would be better off with more of these people on their payrolls. Unfortunately, too many managers still operate from some personal need to *control* other people rather than from a genuine desire to maximize productive output. (Some exceptions will be found in Chapter 14.)

Any person who has had the experience of working in both a small organization (under 20 employees) and a large one is likely to have noticed that certain business practices that are regarded as rather obvious common-sense matters in the small work group tend to be given fancy designations and to take on a certain rigidity when found in the big company or government bureaucracy. A case in point is something that has come to be called

Flextime

Here we have a management practice which, to put it simply, allows to some extent for the fact that different employees have different life circumstances that make it inconvenient for them to arrive at and depart from the workplace at precisely the same time as everybody else.

Most small work organizations have always understood that such trivial matters as the arrival and departure times of employees were considerations that could easily be adjusted to the priorities of high performance and productivity and have acted accordingly. Unfortunately, until quite recently, very few large organizations had operated in this common-sense manner. (I speak here of North America. Flextime has been common practice in several European countries for more than a decade.)

Thus we now have teams of consultants engaged in a painfully slow process of educating our private and public bureaucracies in the benefits of flexible arrival and departure times. (In rare instances flextime even includes the possibility of a two-hour lunch break for secretaries, just as their bosses have.) All this expense and confusion, even though nearly every organization that has implemented flextime has soon reported direct benefits in terms of reduction of lost work time, improved employee morale, and increased productivity. (See Research and Resource Information at the end of the book.)

In general I view flextime as a kind of fine-tuning of basically bureaucratic management, not a *major* departure from the 9 to 5 mode. After all, how different really is 7 to 3 or 10 to 6? Helpful, certainly *necessary*, but not all that *different*. It does begin to feel different, though, when the two-hour lunch break is one of the possibilities. Because in Chicago in the summertime, you can get to Oak Street Beach in ten minutes from most downtown offices. If most of us had time to do our shopping in the daytime, stores wouldn't have to use up all that energy staying open at night.

But, so far, the standard flextime arrangement is something less than a major departure. The same could be said of part-time work, if attention were paid to the traditional definition and severe limitations of most part-time jobs. The pattern is clear. Rarely does a part-time job carry much responsibility. It is even rarer that it leads to significant personal advancement. All too often, compensation for the part-time job fails even to include adequate fringe benefits in its compensation.

Thanks to the work of vigorous organizations such as New Ways to Work, the National Council for Alternative Work Patterns, and Workshare, traditional employers are being encouraged to improve the quality and compensation of part-time jobs as a way of gaining the skills and talents of people who cannot, or choose not to, work on a full-time basis.

In any case, in this book, it will not be the usual kinds of part-time jobs we will be exploring. The category here is better defined as

Working Less Than Full Time

There is a big difference. Working less than full-time describes the work pattern of a person who takes three months of free time each year as well as the person who works three hours each day. We could speak of "the four-day week," but how would we encompass the person who works four days one week, six the next, and none the third? In this book we are exploring *unconventional* work arrangements, usually with workdays and hours determined by the individual rather than the employer.

In the pages that follow we will share the experiences of a management consultant who, for the most part, works a full day, but can usually take a few weeks off several times a year; a commodities trader who works, for money, two hours each weekday; a convention-service person with a totally unpredictable work schedule; and a man who has several sources of income, each of which could be considered a part-time job.

Part-time work also happens to be of direct importance to the quality of our lives in a way that most of us would never think of. Part-time jobs constitute one of the most essential support systems for all of the fine arts in any industrialized culture. Most of our musicians, painters, sculptors, actors, independent film and video producers, and writers have spent years working part-time as waiters, cab drivers, secretaries, receptionists, models, or messengers, as they have gradually refined their artistic skills. (One of the people who helped me with the typing of this manuscript is a very competent and original sculptor, Terry Rumble. She has also worked at a number of other part-time jobs to support her two children.)

Many "established" people in the arts still hold some other part-time job, especially those with families to provide for. I am impressed by the high level of skill and integrity these people deliver in performing these supposedly low-status jobs. It seems that some of them even come to value these occasions for involvement in "the real world" as a source of enrichment for their art.

One of the most exciting and constructive developments in the area of working less than full-time is the concept of

Job Sharing

The benefits to any employer of hiring two part-time people instead of one full-time person to perform a set of tasks are so clear that it is hard to understand why this mode of organizing work is only now being tentatively tried out in a handful of work organizations in North America. With very few exceptions, in every place that has implemented job sharing, productivity and employee morale have gone up and lateness and absenteeism have nearly disappeared. An excellent survey of this development can be found in the book *Job Sharing: A New Pattern for Quality of Work and Life,* by Gretl S. Meier.

So far we have described situations in which time is the essential variable. But many people—increasing numbers in recent years it seems—insist that their range of personal choice in the matter of their work must go beyond simply control of their own time. These people want to determine *where* they will work as well as *when,* and prefer to set their own compensation rates and put together their own fringe benefits, if any. These are the

Free-Lancers and Consultants

Many people who have performed well in some service role in an organization have reached a point where they might have said, "I could do this just as well on my own— and probably make more money." In recent years the tag line may more often be, ". . . and have a lot more free time." (As we shall see in Chapter 4, there is a notable increase in the number of people who prefer more free time to more money.)

Some years ago if you were called self-employed it meant that you owned some kind of small business. But now, large numbers of people are finding a comfortable middle ground between working for some organization and all the complications of running a business. These are the free-lancers and consultants. Their numbers are legion. It has been suggested that one-third of the people in Washington, D.C., for example, are bureaucrats, one-third lobbyists, and the rest "consultants." Every university community has a group of veteran grant chasers who are available to do "research" on short-term projects. The magazine industry could not survive without the intrepid free-lance writers; and one of our biggest growth industries in recent years, the entertainment business, is staffed in large part by self-employed men and women—actors, directors, camera technicians, musicians, dancers, managers, and more. Some of these people choose to organize their days and weeks and years as closely as possible along the lines of the traditional "regular" job—one way of establishing and maintaining the self-discipline essential for this kind of life. But many self-employed people lead lives that are created day by day. Scot Gardiner, who divides his work time between a part-time research job in Montreal, free-lance writing in the village of Alcove, Quebec, and a fair amount of traveling and consulting, literally "designs" each day as he goes along.

As we have mentioned, many people are as concerned with *where* they work as with other factors, and for many there is a special joy in

Working at Home

Although certainly not for everyone, some people find working at home the most efficient and/or enjoyable way to get things done. Others find it a way to integrate the various dimensions of their lives—work, family, other interests. Many creative artists and writers find that inspiration comes at unpredictable moments and need to have the tools of their craft available at all times.

Alvin Toffler in *The Third Wave* envisions a future not so far off where many people may be performing highly sophisticated work in their homes with the help of home-computer consoles, video and word-processing equipment, and other as yet undiscovered technologies. Several of our interview subjects are already operating on the basis of Toffler's "electronic cottage" model. And even a few major corporations are beginning to discover that it is not necessary for all their employees to commute to a central workplace and take up expensive downtown office space. We'll learn more about these interesting departures in Chapter 14.

Working at home is certainly nothing new. Some of the most important contributions to our civilization were developed in someone's spare room. We have only to recall Thomas Edison, Pablo Picasso, or John Maynard Keynes, who did half of his typical day's work while still in bed! And before leaving the subject it is certainly worth noting that many a thriving business got its start over someone's kitchen table.

The opposite fantasy to that of working at home is the footloose travel fantasy. There have always been people who wanted to see the world, or at least part of it. They find their special satisfaction in

Work You Can Do Anywhere

Certain skills, experience, and knowledge can be exchanged for money almost anywhere. An experienced real estate salesman can function just as well in Cleveland or Albuquerque. A talented computer programmer can find short-term jobs, or a permanent career, in Brussels or Buenos Aires as well as Boston or San Diego. At the present time nurses are needed everywhere. And if you are a really good chef you will have lucrative offers wherever you go.

One of my acquaintances happens to know how to repair dry-cleaning equipment. It's kind of a nasty job, but this fellow can arrive in his van in any city and within hours find enough work to keep him busy for several weeks. And he earns enough so he can take a lot of time off between jobs. His way of working is not untypical of that of many of the people in the following pages. He knows his craft and chooses to apply it on *his* terms, *when* he wants to and *where* he wants to.

Then there's one more category of unco
arrangement that we might as well call

All of the Above

Once people discover that they can function effectively
without heavy structure imposed by someone else (and we
must remember that some can't or prefer not to), they
often gradually come to realize that life can get very interesting when you have the flexibility to do more than organize your whole life around a standard job.

Mary Grace is a case in point. When I interviewed her
she was sharing a hospital job with another person and
running a consulting business from her home. She works a
lot of hours—because she wants to. On the other hand, Jay
Levinson always has at least a half-dozen different ways of
earning money going simultaneously, typically working
three to four days a week, usually at home.

The fact is that among the people I interviewed, most of
those who had been away from 9 to 5 jobs for a long time
had more than one way of earning income. But always *on
their own terms*. Some call it "working free."

3

Why People Leave Traditional Jobs

The way in which work is defined in our society, the way in which it's organized, structured, rewarded, and withheld, is one of the main generators of social and mental health problems.

—Elliot Liebow
Director, Center for Work and
Mental Health
National Institute of Mental
Health

Why are so many people dissatisfied with traditional jobs? What is the significance of so much dissatisfaction? A social scientist or policymaker might be interested in attitudes as precursors of social trends. One could hope that employers might discover in these reasons for dissatisfaction some things that could be changed in their own organizations, thereby improving stability, employee morale, and productivity. Many readers may be feeling stirrings of discontent themselves and wondering if there is something wrong with *them* instead of the work situation, wondering whether their feelings of frustration are legitimate, shared by others.

The reasons for making a change to a more autonomous

work situation that are discussed in the following pages come from two sources. The first is the workshop I conducted in the summer of 1980 on the subject "Inventing Your Own Job." The 150 participants in the workshop came from a wide range of occupations and professions. All were asked to write down their reasons for wanting to leave a traditional job situation. The result was an extraordinary collection of brief, pointed messages. If one thing was clear from this workshop, it was that people seemed to know exactly what it was they were dissatisfied with, and could state it succinctly and forcefully. The second source is in-depth interviews with about 50 people, most of whom have made a change from some traditional job to a more flexible or autonomous (or both) work arrangement. (A few of our interview subjects have *never* had the experience of working at a "regular" job.)

The reasons people give for wanting to leave jobs tend to fall into five categories, although several concerns often overlap to a considerable extent. In general, though, people leave or wish to leave traditional jobs for the following major reasons: (1) dissatisfaction with the nature of the work itself, expressed in such complaints as "not making the best use of my talents," "boring work," and so on; (2) lack of opportunity for personal growth or significant advancement in a desired direction—"This is a dead-end job," or "I feel stifled where I am now"; (3) a desire for greater personal freedom—"I have important things to do besides work and need more free time," or "I just don't work well on someone else's schedule"; (4) a perceived need for more money; and (5) a desire to change locations—"I've had enough of the big city," or "I want to live in a warm climate." Of course, people have many dimensions and highly complex motivations and may have countless other reasons that do not fit accurately into any of these categories.

The order of the above reasons for dissatisfaction reflect

"*Let's see, your schedule for today, as I have it, says you will arrive at the office late, glance through your mail, leave immediately for lunch, and never return, ever.*"

Drawing by Stan Hunt; ©1979
The New Yorker Magazine, Inc.

only the ranking of the reasons given by the people in my survey. But we shall see in the next chapter that a number of recent attitude surveys on this subject, conducted according to scientific methods, show results largely congruent with those described here.

The most important general finding, in my opinion, is

that *the traditional notion of financial compensation as the main factor in work motivation simply doesn't hold up.* The top three complaints have to do with limitations on the individual, *most of which a perceptive manager could do something about that would not cost money.* Indeed, it is a fact that work organizations which make it a point to maximize employees' autonomy, flexibility, and personal growth often enjoy lower turnover and higher employee morale and productivity, which, if other aspects of management are competent, usually results in improved earnings. (See Research and Resource Information.)

But let us listen now to some real people with some real complaints. First, the one-liners from our workshop:

"Seeking freedom from the chains of command."

"Need for built-in change, growth."

"No room for creativity in the corporate structure."

"Lack of recognition for creativity and excellence."

"Lack of independence and sense of accomplishment."

"Greater use of my own skills."

"I need to get out of the kitchen—to escape intolerable pressures of the job."

"I wish to run my own life."

"I can't accept the values and lifestyle demanded by my career. Monetary 'success' is no longer so important."

"I'm smothering!"

"Don't like others controlling my time."

"I want to use my energy more productively to advance my own life rather than company aims."

"I want to improve and grow beyond what I've been 'trained' for."

"Disgusted with management."

"Wanted new challenge, new material—was feeling stagnant."

Many people used the word "challenge" to identify an

important missing factor in their work. Another major
yearning was for "variety." This included "variety of
careers," "variety of viewpoints," and of course the many
references to "boredom" are another way of noting too
much of one thing. One person said, "I have been doing
the same sort of work for 15 years. I love it but feel that a
change would be exciting and stimulating."

Here it is appropriate to call attention to an excellent
survey of psychological studies of motivation in relation to
work that can be found in Tibor Scitovsky's book, *The
Joyless Economy*. Scitovsky's overview of the research documents the fact that variety and stimulation are as important to people as comfort and security. In fact, most people
are restless, according to Scitovsky, without an appropriate
balance between comfort and stimulation. Perhaps if more
managers understood this basic human need—and re-
sponded to it—fewer people would find the need to make
plans to leave the established work organizations.

All of this could, mistakenly, be read as merely another
manifestation of the so-called "me" generation—excessive
preoccupation with self. This is, however, an erroneous
interpretation, for the simple reason that the kind of work
one does and the social organization of that work have
always been powerful shapers of people's feelings of self-
worth. One respondent articulated this clearly: "I felt frustrated and had a very low self-image. I needed a job I felt
good about to feel good about me—so I could grow."
Another gave as his reasons for transition, "establishing
independence and building up my self-worth."

A healthy degree of self-esteem is one of the most fundamental requisites for human happiness, and must not be
confused with selfishness. It is interesting that at least a
few of our respondents expressed a definite interest in
serving others—even a big corporation! In fact, the second
reason for making a change given by the person who ex-

pressed a low self-image was, "I wanted to do something worthwhile for others." And while one person gave as his most important reason for wanting a career change "gut dissatisfaction with the corporate scene," another said, "I'm a job mismatch at General Motors. I'd like to learn how to solve this problem and still remain within the corporation in a personally satisfying and creative manner. I want to help GM."

Money was considered an issue by only a handful of the people in the workshop. It was the *primary* reason for change of only two. Usually, when the money issue was raised there were several other important issues ahead of it. For example, one person who gave as a second reason, "increasing my earning power," a reasonable enough desire, said his primary motivation was toward "more flexibility with respect to my own time." Another person listed six different reasons adding "$$" as the seventh.

Sometimes even the expressed interest in money seemed to reveal something more important, as, for example, in the person who wanted "to be financially independent and avoid a cutthroat environment." Another wanted "an increase in income and rewards that are intrinsic and satisfying." I will repeat the second part—*and rewards that are intrinsic and satisfying*—because it gets at the very crux of the subject of this book. To put it as simply as possible, people are seeking substantial changes in the part of their lives devoted to work because of *internal distresses*. For too many people, our work systems are incompatible with their basic needs and fundamental values. The importance to an individual of deriving feelings of self-worth, of having the opportunity to express creativity, of seeking personal growth or variety of experience—in short, the primary motivations of most people in affluent societies—are inadequately understood and badly handled in too many of our traditional work organizations.

A recent article by Judith Miller in the business section of the Sunday *New York Times* states the problem clearly:

> Despite half-hearted efforts by a few businesses to encourage employees and junior executives either to challenge existing corporate practices and procedures, or to propose daring innovations that could enhance efficiency and profit, most corporations, management experts agree, remain largely inflexible, autocratically run entities resistant to change and to the "better idea." In fact such business-as-usual is so much the norm that a company's efforts to involve employees and lower-echelon executives in decision making still attract considerable attention.

We will have more to say about a few of those attention-getting exceptions in our chapter "Some Enlightened Employers."

So far in this chapter we have presented only some top-of-the head reasons for leaving traditional jobs for something more satisfying. Let's listen now to a few people describing that decision to break away in more detail. We begin with two classic cases of people who climbed the corporate ladder very successfully.

The first one moved all the way from a lowly receptionist position. She is Patricia Lee, currently working as an independent consultant on job sharing and other flexible work options, based in Manhattan. In the process of hearing her story, you may discover a number of clues as to how an intelligent person in a series of 9 to 5 jobs gains the kind of experience and knowledge that eventually makes it possible for her to work on her own terms.

"At my first job I was a receptionist trainee with Allied Chemical. I got promoted to secretary in the personnel department soon after I started. I worked in that spot for two years, and then the company moved to New Jersey. Then for another two years I was a secretary for Oakite

Products in technical services. I left there to go to the American Management Associations as administrative assistant to the director of research and information services.

"I felt I was moving up in the world. I had a lot of exposure to business theory and management at that point because we were in information, and I'd finally gotten past the secretarial rung. Eventually, though, I decided I wanted to get out of New York for a while, and I quit that job to go to England. When I returned, homesick for New York after two months, I got a job pretty much right away as administrative assistant to the director of marketing at U.S. Plywood, where I spent the next ten and a half years.

"When I started, my boss was director of marketing services. Every time I'd start getting bored, he'd get a promotion. I kept moving up with him—you know, vice-president of this and vice-president of that, president of a division. . . . At the same time I had this parallel voluntary career with the alumni association of International House for students in New York. I was at various times secretary, vice-president, president. I ran their summer houses for a few years, winter houses, clothing bank . . . did a lot of cooking during that time.

"And then, about the time I was getting bored as administrative assistant, my boss began looking for a special assistant to handle special projects. At the same time, I was offered a job at International House in community relations. I went to my boss and told him that while I didn't particularly want to leave the company, I did want to do something that was my own as opposed to being his right hand. He offered me the new spot! For a year I held that job and, among other things, planned the management meetings. Then the man who was in charge of administrative services moved into a writing slot, and I was promoted into that job, which incorporated manager of administrative services with my other job. So I was still in charge of meetings and special projects, but also in charge of some personnel work, administrative services, space planning, policies and procedures manuals, organization manuals, budgeting for contributions, and word processing.

"While doing that, someone came to us for contributions for a drug program. About a year later U.S. Plywood decided to move to Connecticut. At the same time the people at the drug program needed somebody to help them get a women's program started, and they asked me if I would be willing to do it on a volunteer basis. So when Plywood moved to Connecticut, I decided not to go with them, and took the severance pay I was entitled to—26 weeks, or whatever it was. Anyhow, it was a lot of severance pay.

"About six months before I left Plywood, I decided I really could live on less money—that I didn't really need to buy everything at Bloomingdale's, and that I didn't need a $150-a-month garage for my car. I could manage to park it on the street if I used a little time looking. So I spent that six months investigating every angle on how to live more cheaply. I made a game out of it. Trying to live on less money so I could 'indulge' myself in this volunteer work that was very near and dear to my heart. The issue was one that had been of major importance to me all of my life. I think that was the beginning of my breaking out of traditional work styles."

Since then, Pat's work life has consisted mainly of a series of consulting or special-projects jobs, part-time jobs—even some temporary-help jobs, which she says give her important information about how different companies do things. And her pleasant, comfortable, Upper East Side apartment is a long way from poverty, as well as a short, convenient walk to many of her business clients.

One thing that happens for some people in large business firms is that they come to a realization that they could do the same thing they are doing, or something similar, on their own, without the boss and the big organization. It happened to me in 1966 when I left Rand McNally's college textbook division after eight years to start my own book publishing company. It also happened to Bob Marriott, who once had a very successful career in big-league advertising and now earns a handsome living working in partnership with his wife, Jane, in their San Francisco home as a marketing consultant to restaurants.

Jane had been doing a lot of free-lance art work for advertising agencies, including the one Bob worked for. Asked about whether any one thing precipitated their decision to strike out on their own, she said, "No, there was nothing special. The only thing I could point to that might have been a landmark was that Bob had been in the agency business for years and he turned 40. He seemed to make a decision then and said to me, 'I don't think I want to work for anyone else anymore.'"

Bob's version: "Three and a half years ago we moved here from Chicago and started our consulting business, but I had known for at least a year or more before that I had definitely had enough of the advertising agency business as such, and that I really didn't want to work for anybody else anymore. In that business, satisfying your clients, I think, is enough. To have to satisfy your boss *and* your client is like serving two masters. Most people do it. I wondered if there was something a little peculiar about me, because I found after 18 years that I just didn't like it anymore."

Pressed to be a bit more specific about his discontent, Bob Marriott shared some of his work history:

"I was with several advertising agencies. My last five years I was running the Chicago office of a medium-size ($15 million) agency. When I started with the agency, two of us opened that Chicago office—on the understanding that the other fellow who brought me in was eventually going to run the company, and I would run the Chicago office. And that pretty much was the way it turned out to be.

"We started out with two of us and a secretary, and over a period of three or four years we built it up to about 25 people. It was a going concern. I was made executive vice-president of the agency, and eventually was going to be president, and all that sort of thing. I enjoyed it during the first couple of years, up to the point where we had about ten people. But the bigger it got, the less I liked it. The bigger it got, the more I became an administrator and a manager of an office rather than someone who was dealing day to day with clients, dealing with problems, and creating solutions to those problems. I thought at the time that maybe I was an adequate administrator, but I really knew I was better at being an account manager and creator. And there just wasn't enough time to do what I thought I did best.

"At the agency I had been doing a lot of work with clients in the hotel and restaurant field—a very wide range of clients from Mr. Donut to Howard Johnson's, Holiday Inn, the Jacques chain of fine restaurants out of Chicago, and another chain of cafeterias and fast-food operations. I began to feel that I had finally gotten experience in so many areas of the restaurant and hotel field that I probably knew more about it than almost anybody in the business. It had happened kind of accidentally. I had kind of just fallen into this deal with restaurants and hotels, and liked it, and became so entirely involved with it.I really did know everything there was to know, at least from the marketing and promotion side. So I looked around and said, 'You know, there doesn't seem to be anybody out there specializing in this field, and it looks like a lot of people need specialized help rather than just the broad-based advertising agency approach to marketing.' I felt the restaurant and hotel field was just sort of waiting for somebody to come along and do this. I dared myself: 'Why not take a chance and see if it's true?'"

Judging from the quality of life enjoyed these days by Bob and Jane Marriott, it was true. One thing we learn from this story is that boredom or discontent with a job, even a very good job, can lead to a creative leap ahead to a much better life provided you can spot the special opportunities where special knowledge and skills can be used to advantage.

Some people leave 9 to 5 jobs because their own nervous systems do not function best between those specific hours. It seems only natural to them that they should work when they are at their best, rather than when they are not even fully awake.

Francine Rizzo, an extremely creative, highly productive consultant in the field of information systems, explains: "I had a 9 to 5 job for many years and always found it very difficult to get there on time, because I am not a morning person. And that's one of the reasons I started my own business in New York. When I get up in the morning I like to read the paper and relax over a cup of coffee. I've always liked to talk to people on the phone. I like to sit outside when I want to. I like not to have to worry about being somewhere, not to have to buck traffic to get there. I just don't like to have to be somewhere at a certain time." Some people are likely to view this attitude as irresponsible. But Francine's clients—firms like Safeway stores and the Crocker Bank—certainly don't find her irresponsible. They're extremely pleased with the work she does for them. Consulting is one of those ways of working where a person gets paid for the work that gets done rather than for being somewhere during certain fixed hours.

At age 36, Terry Mollner has been through two career

fields, both of which gave him a lot of satisfaction and success, and he is currently engaged in several different kinds of work, only one of which produces significant income and none of which has to do with any "career" track. Terry currently earns his living by spending two hours each weekday trading commodities for a group of investors through his Mollner Commodity Fund. Terry is also a part-time consultant to not-for-profit organizations and is executive director of the Trusteeship Institute, which has the purpose, among other things, of setting up new businesses in which the employees are the owners and the managers.

Terry's first career was as a high school drama teacher. He described for me his transition from working in the context of a traditional institution to his first round of "working free":

"I taught theater, and I loved it. I was very, very good at teaching high school kids. But I was also experimental and ran my classroom as a democracy, so there were lots of problems. The principal turned against me for really wrong reasons. I ended up making my democracies very successful—two rock groups and some very good actors and debaters came out of my classrooms. But it scared the hell out of the other speech teachers. So I quit teaching high school and began to run groups because I enjoyed psychology and working with people and helping people to interact and grow. And I knew all along that what I was really trying to do was help myself grow. I was maybe more honest about that than some psychologists are. I learned a lot through the groups and did it for many years."

Terry's entirely self-taught venture into commodities trading has experienced the usual ups and downs of that unpredictable business, but on the whole he has done very well.

Some people nurture a conscious fantasy about what they really want to be doing with their lives—a fantasy that is often greatly at odds with a traditional sort of job. Art Ritchie was an administrator in a hospital with a special love for carving wood. Not yet 30, his plan for the future was to work in the hospital for five to ten years and carefully save enough money so that he would eventually be able to quit and just do his woodcarving. But he began encountering old men who had once had similar ideas— "work a few years, save money, start my own business"— and these men, now in their sixties or seventies, were to Art's dismay still at the old routines. These conversations jolted Ritchie into making a decision not to postpone moving into doing exactly what he wanted to do. He also indicated that "having too many bosses" was an additional motivation.

Art was quick to teach himself the fundamentals of carving and eventually line up enough commercial business— carving signs and plaques—to bring in an income that allowed him to take the time to do the creative, one-of-a-kind wood sculptures that give him real satisfaction.

The people we have talked about so far have all had very clear reasons for making a move from a standard, more or less 9 to 5 job to some looser work arrangement, and their versions of the differences between the two work styles tend to be in sharp contrast. The issue gets more complex for other people.

One such person is Betsy Barley, a highly talented and successful writer and editor in the medical field. Betsy sees advantages to both a regular job and free-lancing—very different advantages, to be sure. As a result, her career of over 20 years has been characterized by long periods of holding a regular job as a writer or editor for such publications as *Good Housekeeping* and *Medical World News,* alternating with periods of a year or two of free-lance writing.

It is perhaps worth noting that this possibility of moving back and forth from a well-paying, stable job to free-lancing is one of the rewards of doing what you do with a very high level of competence—perhaps the ultimate "security" in the world of work.

Betsy's description of her choices gives us a richer picture of some of the factors we have uncovered with the other people interviewed and the kinds of trade-offs involved in shifting from one mode of work to another:

"Almost all of the regular jobs I've held in the past have been strictly reporting or editing for magazines. And I'm beginning to realize that that's one of the best of all possible worlds to work in. You have a product that must get out. You have a group of people willing to work to put that product out. And unless for some reason it's an unusual, hostile environment, you have good working relationships. I did work for one magazine where the atmosphere was really *cold,* but at every other place I've worked, you're more or less a team, and I think that's a great advantage. It's a lot of fun working with people to put out an issue. And I've always had a great deal of respect for myself as a reporter and an editor. I don't always have the same kind of feeling for other projects I've done.

"The way I've approached free-lancing is as a way to just not have to go into an office every day. And for that I love it! I really do like my free time, my spare time, but the disadvantage is that you don't get as much responsibility as you do when you're on the job."

Betsy knows herself pretty well and has learned what she likes and doesn't like in a work situation:

"The only thing I was really unhappy with was being in an editing position for three and a half years which meant that I literally had to be there at 9 o'clock and didn't leave until 6 or 7 o'clock seven days a week, and I had to be *there* all the time. Whereas in reporting, I was out a lot, and I could arrive at work at 10 if I wanted to. I really had a great deal of freedom. I haven't had negative work experiences as much as many other people have. But then I've never tried to rise in a corporation either, and I've never been that competitive."

On one occasion Betsy had a special reason for leaving a job. She relates, "I went into free-lancing that time as a way of taking another job that I really didn't know if I wanted, and it was a way to buy some time to do my other projects." Whether working for someone else or on her own, Betsy seems well grounded in a sensible acceptance of the realities of life: "It's O.K. I think that work is work is work. And if you enjoy it, that's terrific!"

Michael Hassan recently left a long and successful career in radio in the Midwest and moved to New England to share his life with Carol Raney and her daughter, Brooke, and to start an independent video-production business. At this stage, Mike and Carol are a little like free-lance writers, but with video equipment instead of typewriters as the hardware involved.

In Mike's case, the decision to leave a secure job as manager of a radio station is enmeshed in a complex set of interrelated decisions and considerations having to do with what are two major life themes for many people: the desire for a full and satisfying close relationship with another person (in this case two other persons) and the sort of reevaluation of priorities many men experience as they approach middle age, or the "midlife crisis." The degree to which such a reevaluation is in fact a crisis has a lot to do with how well a person knows himself and what resources he has to work with. In Mike's case it seems more like a well-thought-out transition than a crisis, even though big risks were being undertaken.

I asked Mike about his motivations for making the change from a stable job to the life of a free-lance video producer, a field which is entirely new to him (though not to Carol):

"That's a pretty complex question. There are a lot of motivations. Money is one. It is not, in this case, the most important one. That's one of the things I think that's nice about working for yourself. It is also an attempt to answer the question: 'Can two people with divergent careers put it together and live together and work together?' I think that's a very valid motivation that people are facing and acting on more and more these days. The time when a man could say, 'Well, I've got to go live in a certain place because my job says so,' is just not there anymore. The challenge of doing something new is a motivation. The idea of making something work is a motivation. Some combination of all of these things plus probably a few things that I'm not even aware of.

"I would also say that Carol and I have some motivations that are different—some of them are the same, but others are different. I guess for me one of the things would be that I spent so long working in one field that, you know, you get to the stage where you want to test yourself. And you say, 'I've done pretty well at this particular thing, but I grew up in it, and if I can't do well at it, I probably ought to go out and slash my wrists. Can I do well at something else?' I think that's probably a pretty important motivation. I would say that I was fortunate in that at my age I have both the time and some money to be able to indulge those questions. It's not something that everybody has the opportunity to do.

"I was married for ten years, and was divorced a few years ago. With that, and a reexamination of where I was and what I was doing, and thinking that now my needs are different, asking where my responsibilities lie, . . . and a lot of other things. So part of it is an attempt to answer those questions."

Some of the reasons people give for leaving standard jobs are pretty far out. Ludwig Henkel says the main reason he left a full-time job in Toronto after many years to set up a small home-based business in the country was the *parking problem!* Barbara Keck left an excellent job in marketing management at Continental Can for a reason shared by many women—she had a baby. She would have preferred to continue her work on a part-time basis, but the company said no. So Barbara started her own consulting firm and works three days a week, mostly at home. "My first priority is my family," she says, "and my boss—me—understands that."

4

Values, Attitudes, Priorities, and Motivation

Women have always wanted meaningful work helping people instead of money, power, or prestige. In the future men, too, will enjoy the luxury of choosing work for the intrinsic value of doing it.

—Caroline Bird
The Two Paycheck Marriage

The world of work in North America as we enter the 1980s is a world of paradoxes with many crosscurrents of change. In recent years, American industry has provided a remarkably steady increase in the number of new available jobs. During the same period, our national unemployment figures have also steadily increased. Women demand responsible jobs in the general economy, at the same time they demand large blocks of time off for giving birth and caring for children. The sons of factory workers get engineering degrees or MBAs at Harvard, Stanford, or Carnegie-Mellon, while some sons of Wall Street executives earn their living as carpenters or social workers. The rank and file of labor unions, long the boiling pot of radical social change, have become the conservative middle class, demanding lower taxes and less government. Young heirs

40

of great wealth agonize about how to find "meaningful" work.

Men become "house husbands," Ph.D.'s drive cabs—all the old rules of the work-status-income game seem to have gone up in smoke, with the result that more people have more options, and therefore have to make many more choices about the role of work in their lives. Only one thing hasn't changed. If you ask a good cross-section of people how they feel about their work, you will still get every conceivable kind of answer, from the elation of creative, productive people who truly love their work, to the frustration, anger, or passivity of the unfulfilled, to the despair of the chronically unemployed.

Social scientists have systematically questioned people on how they feel about their work ever since the techniques of survey research were developed in the 'thirties and 'forties; and, as the nature of most people's work and their attitudes toward it have changed over the years, so have the questions and answers. Now, after years of confusing patterns of values and feelings, a clear, strong new trend in people's attitudes toward work is being documented: Whereas once it seemed that nearly everyone was willing to overlook a lot of boredom, frustration, or unhealthy working conditions for the sake of more and more money and the possessions and status that come with money, we now find a dramatic increase in concern for such things as quality of working life and, especially, greater personal freedom. "Working free" in one form or another seems to have become an important life goal for large and increasing numbers of North Americans.

The flavor of this new wave can be found in the results of recent surveys by the research firm Yankelovich, Skelly & White, summarized in the book *Work in America: The Decade Ahead.* In this report, Yankelovich, impressed by dramatic changes in the values and attitudes of many working people in recent years, coined the phrase "New Breed" to describe those people (a slight majority now, he believes) for whom the traditional values of money, status, achievement, and "success" are no longer the ruling factors in their lives. When these fundamental values change, the purpose and value accorded to work also change:

> For the New Breed, family and work have grown less important and leisure more important. When work and leisure are compared as sources of satisfaction, only one out of five people (21 percent) state that work means more to them than leisure. The majority (60 percent) say that while they enjoy their work, it is not their major source of satisfaction. (The other 19 percent are so exhausted by the demands work makes of them that they cannot conceive of it as even a minor source of satisfaction.)

Yankelovich goes on to cite a recent study in Sweden that confirms the fact that this fundamental value shift is not just an American phenomenon.

Another recent study, sponsored by the National Commission for Manpower Policy, brings the matter down to specifics with some rather surprising findings. Fred Best, reporting the results of a survey of public employees, says, "Workers may be willing to exchange earnings for more free time, and they favor increased flexibility in the timing of education, work, and leisure." For example, in one survey people were asked whether they would prefer an opportunity for more pay or more free time. "Specifically, the first choice of the large group (40.8 percent) went to 25 days of additional vacation, but only a slightly smaller 32.3 percent chose the 10 percent pay raise first." Summarizing that survey, Best says,

> 48.5 percent of the respondents were willing to give up at least some of their income for more vacation time. More

specifically, 21 percent of the respondents stated that they would give up 2 percent of current income for one added week of vacation, 12 percent would exchange 5 percent of income for 12.5 added days of vacation, 8.1 percent would exchange 10 percent for 25 days, and 7.4 percent would exchange 20 percent for 50 days.

On the other hand, we have the recent "Playboy Report on the American Male,"* based on a Louis Harris survey of U.S. males between the ages of 18 and 49. In the category headed "evaluating job rewards," the Harris group found "a good salary" chosen as most important by 56 percent of those polled, with "job security" the next most important consideration for 50 percent. Only 16 percent placed a high value on "freedom to decide how you do the job," and only 23 percent ranked "having enough free time to enjoy other things" near the top of their list. Undoubtedly a survey that included women would show different priorities.

There are two *fundamentally different ways to view work:* one, which could be called the institutional viewpoint, regards institutions as most important, whether we're talking about the national economy, the corporation, the government bureaucracy, or the school or hospital. In other words, the *context* of work is the key to understanding the institutional viewpoint.

This perspective carries its own special view of motivation. The individual working person's motivation according to the institutional viewpoint tends to be *extrinsic.* That is, the assumption is that human beings are motivated by something external to themselves, whether it be accumulation of money and posssessions, or achieving goals set by someone else, or working for the sake of the family, or

*"Playboy Report on the American Male," *Playboy,* February 1979.

meeting parents' expectations. In short, the institutional view asserts that people work because there are things "out there" that must be taken care of.

If we can say that this institutional view is a kind of "outside-in" view, the alternative then is an "inside-out" view. Accordingly, people work because of *intrinsic* motivation. There is something inside people that moves them to be creative and productive. This intrinsic motivation can range from a very simple requirement of the human organism to eat and to be protected from the elements (survival), to what might be called a spiritual view of work motivation, in which the person feels a need in the world that he or she is particularly well suited to fill. Or a person may feel "called" to a vocation. It may simply be a powerfully felt need for self-expression, for making one's mark in the world. In such cases of intrinsic motivation, the major reward may very well be in the accomplishment of the work itself.*

The writer of the "Playboy Report on the American Male" concludes:

> Intrinsic work satisfactions are obviously of paramount importance to American men. Five of the 15 items ranked "very important" relate to rewards to be found on the job itself. "A chance to use your mind and abilities" ranks the highest, with four out of five men (79 percent) stressing its importance. Similarly, "doing meaningful things" and "a chance for personal growth" are rated third and fifth, respectively, with two men in three describing them as very important.

In this book, although we accept the validity and the importance of the institutional view (without it we would

*Some very interesting experimental work has been done by Mihaly Csikszentmihalyi of the University of Chicago clarifying the difference between extrinsic and intrinsic motivation. See especially his book *Beyond Boredom and Anxiety*.

not have any enduring institutions), we focus primarily on the intrinsic view, since we are talking by and large about people who have chosen a path of some considerable independence from institutions.

An overview of dominant attitudes spanning the past 30 years would seem to support the notion of a trend toward intrinsic values. In the 1950s, books such as *The Organization Man** and *The Man in the Gray Flannel Suit†* clearly documented the tendency of the majority to fit themselves and their motivations and purposes into existing organizations of one sort or another. The family was still a sacred institution, and it was assumed that men, who were the primary or sole breadwinners, would work throughout their lives to further the goals of the corporation and to support their family.

In the 1980s we find more and more people seeking what they call freedom—autonomy, flexibility—in their work lives. And since the work organizations and other institutions of society have been very slow to understand this change in motivation, the people who are determined to move in this direction often find themselves breaking ties with established organizations to do something on their own, or perhaps in the company of a small number of other individuals.

It is worth mentioning here that the subject of work is perhaps second only to education as the most explored subject matter of social science. Thousands of studies and reports have been written on work. Unfortunately, all but a very small number of them approach the subject from the institutional model. They are studies of people functioning in factories, corporate organizations, or govern-

*William H. Whyte, Jr., *The Organization Man*, New York: Simon & Schuster, 1956.

†Sloan Wilson, *The Man in the Gray Flannel Suit*, Cambridge: Bentley, 1980. Originally published in 1955.

ment bureaucracies, responding to the norms and incentive structures of the organization. Until recently very little formal study of work, in which the model of intrinsic motivation is the guiding viewpoint, has been undertaken. The current enthusiasm for Japanese-style management, which encourages employee participation in management decision making, represents a peephole through a door that needs to be opened wider.

Let's look more closely at the distinction between the extrinsic, or institutional, and the intrinsic, or autonomous modes.

People usually grow up with the idea that they will fill a certain position in the economy, whether as teacher, lawyer, business manager, nurse, whatever. The pursuit of this position will typically follow a prescribed educational program that has been well laid out to lead to eventually filling the specified role in society. Once the educational goal has been reached and people begin acting in their chosen roles, the institution itself has ways of taking over individual consciousness (the company man, the Harvard faculty member), reinforcing a certain set of values and behavior over other possible values and actions. Society as a whole strongly reinforces these institutional values.

The standard pattern, then, has been for individuals to accommodate themselves—tailor themselves, if you will—to these institutional roles until the magic age of 65, at which point they are suddenly expected to know how to function outside of the institutional context. The often-noted phenomenon of males dying within a short time after retirement can be explained perhaps in large part by this conditioning.

In contrast, there have always been individuals in society who are uncomfortable in schools, who find it difficult to function at maximum efficiency in the roles and structures imposed by someone else. Cobi Sucher, one of the people interviewed for this book, stated that issue rather force-fully: "I went to college and got a teaching certificate, but somehow or other I couldn't see myself going into any kind of *system*. All my life I have known that the minute I'm put into a system, I begin to get very upset. *I don't like it!*"

Until rather recently the world of the arts was one of the few areas where such individuals could find outlets for their personal energies within a community of similarly motivated persons. As the phenomenon of individuals organizing their work lives on the basis of intrinsic motivations as opposed to fitting into institutional roles increases, it is interesting to observe how closely some people's development of new work patterns and new lifestyles resembles the kinds of work patterns and lifestyles that have been common among artists for centuries. We find, for example, great irregularities in the level of the individual's income; tendencies to live in such a way that the acquisition of money is not a primary motivation; the strong desire often seen among entrepreneurial types and free-lancers to create something new and unique; the tendency of these people to seek the company of other freer spirits, and indeed to create support systems for themselves out of such comradeship.

Let us turn now to our own interview subjects, who, having chosen to reject traditional jobs, explain just what it is that they want—and in most cases are getting—out of their new work arrangements.

It would be easy to assume that a person who doesn't function well within a highly structured system would end up as a dropout, contributing nothing to society. In fact, Cobi Sucher, after raising three children and being widowed at a rather young age, did not look for society to provide her with a means of survival. Instead she looked inside herself. She is a perfect case of intrinsic motivation:

"I started to think back to when I was very young, trying

to remember what I liked to do. When you're three and four years old, you just play and play, right? Then I began to think about being six and nine years old, and then I remembered I played with my dolls constantly. After school I'd line them up and play school. But the one thing I really enjoyed doing was making doll clothes. I did little embroiderings on the doll's dresses. I would knit them little sweaters. I had no patterns. Apparently I could just see this little sweater in my mind, and I just knitted the sweater for the teddy bear or whatever it was.

"And then I realized that was a great talent. At the time it seemed like nothing. I thought, 'Did I really enjoy that?' I had to say yes, I really did. I really enjoyed making those little things. So I said to myself, 'O.K., if you really enjoyed doing those things, why don't you just go back and do it now? Do what you always enjoyed doing.'"

Cobi is now 51 years old, earning a modest but sufficient income working in her home in South Haven, Michigan, creating elegant one-of-a-kind dresses, blouses, skirts, aprons. She described the transition from childhood doll play to her present occupation:

"I started knitting sweaters for grown-ups or grandchildren or whatever, and then started making other things. All of a sudden I said to myself, 'O.K., even if it doesn't pay any money, it doesn't matter, because you're doing what you really want to do. So go ahead and do it.' I kept saying this to myself, and pretty soon I had a lot of clothes for myself all made up. And I can only wear one dress at a time, right? So finally I said, 'Hey, this is ridiculous! I can't use all this stuff myself!' So then I started thinking of selling them, of doing it for other people. And that's how the whole thing got started. The point of all this is that I did go back to the place in my youth when I did things *I really enjoyed doing*. I'm still enjoying it! Every day I love it!"

Cobi works "when I feel like it," which turns out to be

almost every day. But she's also able to take time out for visitors or to ride her bike into town when that's what she feels like doing. And if she wants to take a day or two or a week off, she does.

Doing what you really want to do is perhaps the primary motivation of people who work outside "the system," just as "always working to meet somebody else's goals" is one reason people give for leaving traditional jobs.

Sebastian Moffatt is currently making a good living as an environmental consultant to various agencies of the Canadian government. With a strong background in both theory and practice, his expertise is in constant demand, and he says, "I suppose I could be exploiting it much more if I wanted a career out of it." But he has chosen not to get too involved, for an interesting reason: "I'm frightened to death of getting buried in the bureaucracy, or even just getting killed by the cynicism of the people who work in these bureaucracies." (The final result of too many years working at somebody else's goals?)

Moffatt sees several advantages, in terms of his own values and preferences, in operating as an independent consultant instead of a member of a team: "At least I get to sign my name to what I do. I get to organize my own time and see a process through from beginning to end. So there's a sense of myself in there, of creativity, and a real educational process takes place constantly."

Once again we hear mention of the things so many find missing in traditional jobs—a sense of self-worth, opportunities to be creative, room for personal growth through the work.

I pressed Sebastian Moffatt to elaborate on what gives meaning to his work:

"Well, I've thought about that and struggled with it quite a bit, and I'm still not sure. But my feeling is that the important thing is to have a trade, to look at your work as a

trade. Even if you're doing consulting work on a professional level you should look at it simply as a trade. It's a
service. It's a gift. And the most beautiful thing you can do
with it is to be competent, right? That's what Lao-tsu said,
'Be competent.'"

Mike Pavilon in Chicago left an excellent job with "the
world's largest all-cargo airline" to set up a private therapy
practice and to do management consulting. He said he was
tired of "being locked into having to be accountable every
day to someone, and having to be more concerned with
process than results." Now that he's out on his own, he
seems all energy:

"It struck me in the first few months after leaving how
much more productive I could be as I generated my own
tasks and managed my own time and was strictly accountable for my results. In order to survive, in order to
produce, I had to do things I never did before.

"For survival reasons, and for expression—for expressing myself—I've had to dig, and pick, and choose different
ways to make money. I've learned how to play the stock
market. I have gotten ongoing contracts to do consulting
with chambers of commerce and many small, nonprofit
groups. That hasn't been so challenging or monetarily rewarding, but it's building contacts. We have to devise new
ways of surviving and new ways of expressing ourselves in
order to live the way we want to live." Mike says a lot of this
current motivation and view of life came from a recent
"Outward Bound" excursion, which forced its participants
to take care of themselves in a variety of very challenging
circumstances.

Challenge—another of the factors so many people find
missing in traditional jobs.

Most people who insist on working on their own terms
are pretty good at articulating the values and preferences
that led them to choose this way of life. No one did so

more effectively than Felicia Kaplan, an energetic and highly creative young woman who, like Mike Pavilon, is committed to the good life in Chicago. Felicia earns her living in a wide variety of ways, from free-lance writing to hostessing at private cocktail parties, commercial wine-tasting sessions, temporary office work, and running a very popular workshop she has devised called "Frugal Living"—how to live well on very little money. Felicia knows exactly why she is doing what she is doing:

"I discovered a long time ago that I resist authority, that I don't like to take orders. My father and mother, and my brothers are all in their own businesses, and apparently it's rubbed off on me. I don't want to work for other people. I don't mind working in an office so much if I've gotten the job directly, without the agency." But her preferences are clear: "Actually I detest office work, and I dislike it even more if I'm doing it for somebody else. If I'm going to type, I want to type *my* words, not *theirs*."

Felicia recently spent some time with a career counselor. It would have been fun to be there. At one point the counselor said, "I don't know where you're coming from. I'm not used to dealing with people in nontraditional lifestyles." Felicia said, "That's very obvious. It appears to me you are most comfortable dealing with people in 9 to 5 jobs. All you ever ask me about is how much money I make. Did you ever ask me if I enjoy what I'm doing? Am I happy? Am I achieving some sort of satisfaction? Is it a learning experience? All you ever ask is how much money I make. I'm sick of that! Can't you change your routine a little bit?"

So now, in addition to schools, parents, and bureaucracies to frustrate our most basic motivations, it appears we can add career counselors!

Felicia and I are fighting back. We've both become *non-*career counselors.

5

Risks and Problems

Some people refuse to undertake anything if they have no guarantee that things will work out as they planned. Such people condemn themselves to immobility.
—Jean Monnet
Memoirs

Our examination of the reasons some people have given for leaving standard 9 to 5 jobs, and a deeper probe into values, attitudes, and motivations, provide a clearer picture of the group of working people Daniel Yankelovich has called the New Breed. These are people whose motivation comes mostly from within, who don't like to compromise themselves too much to suit the demands of institutions; people who feel that they are most creative and productive when they are allowed maximum autonomy.

One other characteristic definitively sets the people in this book somewhat apart from the majority. Our people are *risk takers*. But I would immediately qualify that to add that these people are not afraid to take *reasonable* risks. Of course others might view the risks some of them have taken as unreasonable, but that would only be a reflection of *their* values and *their* fears. If we are to understand people who take risks, we must see the risk factors as they see them. It is interesting that, without exception, our interview subjects did not perceive themselves as taking unreasonable risks. It is not that they were unaware of possible problems in doing what they set out to do. Rather, it seems that these people have achieved a basic level of self-confidence, a sense of competence, which makes them feel that they will be able to deal adequately with whatever problems might arise.

I have been intrigued by the difference in attitudes toward risks that I found between two groups: those in my workshop, most of whom had not yet made a change, and those I interviewed. The former group tended to perceive the risks as very great, while the latter often had to be *reminded* that they had taken significant risks. Of course part of that difference is the difference between anticipation and hindsight. We are always more anxious about the unknown. But the other factor—the more important one—is that *it is possible to prepare for risks.*

A person can learn how to minimize risks. Two essential steps are, first and foremost, to *become very good at what you do;* second, *make sure others know of your competence.*

This strategy works even for some people within the context of a traditional organization. Miguel Grinberg is the director of publicity for a major film-distribution company in Buenos Aires, Argentina. He also takes a lot of time off from his job to do other things that interest him, including attending conferences in North America that lure him but that have nothing whatever to do with the work he gets paid for. Miguel says his employer doesn't object, because "I do my job extremely well. They never have anything to complain about. Even if I'm out of town for a while, or out of the office for a few days, they know the work will get done properly."

Betsy Barley did very good work for several different

medical publications and one consumer magazine for many years before becoming a free-lance writer. Terry Mollner carefully taught himself everything he needed to know about the commodities market and tried out his strategy with his own money before inviting others to invest in his fund. Donald Michael built a reputation as a consultant in his field while holding a university professorship, so that when he left the university to become a freelancer, he already had some satisfied clients and a track record. When Bob and Jane Marriott left Chicago to become restaurant consultants in California, they lined up one good client before they made the move. And most of these people had at least a little money saved, fully understanding that the independent work might take time to generate adequate income.

We are talking, essentially, about the difference between a fantasy and a plan. A fantasy without a plan is overflowing with unknown factors and will therefore arouse all sorts of fears. A plan, on the other hand, reduces the number of unknowns.

All this is rather obvious, to be sure. Or should be. Still, some people will leap into a new situation without an adequate assessment of all the relevant factors and a strategy for dealing with them. All too often they fail in what they set out to do. We will have more to say on this subject in Chapter 12. Among other things, we will have some advice from those who have done it.

Some less obvious factors play a part in the perception of risk involved in moving to an autonomous work situation. Again, the contrast between our workshop people and those who have already made the change is interesting. Somehow when a person is considering for the first time the sort of change we are discussing, the possibility of returning to a more structured work situation if the freelancing doesn't work out is often not considered. The explanation is probably because the motivation to be "free" is so strong at that point. But the fact is that people do move back and forth between working for someone else or working full-time, to working on their own or part-time. It is not necessarily a one-way street. In fact, people often find that leaving an unsatisfactory job to work part-time, or on their own, may lead to a much better job later on. In more than one case, for example, Pat Lee's stints as a "temporary" or a "consultant" led to very interesting job offers.

Of course, in dealing with the issue of risk taking, as in most other areas of life, the factor of personality differences cannot be ignored. A person may be extremely competent and a good planner, and may genuinely wish to have more autonomy—yet never do anything about it. Just as some people seem to carry around a lot of anger, some people's first reaction to change of any kind is fear. But it is worth pointing out that even fearful people take risks and often learn to overcome some inappropriate fears in the process. Make Pavilon's experience with "Outward Bound" was a case in point. In fact, overcoming fear is a major goal of that program.

Courage is not one of the traits we acquire in our bureaucratic lifestyles. Risk taking is not encouraged in our schools. We do not have the sort of initiation rites that move adolescents in so-called primitive societies through dangerous confrontations with hard realities so that they may enter adulthood with self-confidence. Most of us work for people who want us to be totally predictable at all times. Unfortunately, if we are ever going to learn how to take sensible risks, we have to teach ourselves. But people do it. Especially people who insist on "working free."

Actually the primary fear most people seem to have when they begin thinking about working on their own, or working less than full time, concerns money, or standard of living. This emerged prominently in our workshop. But it must be understood that very often it is a chosen standard of living that actually limits a person's freedom. Two things became very clear as we discussed this issue with our interview subjects.

First, most people who really want to work on their own terms are prepared to accept a downward adjustment in their incomes—perhaps temporarily, in many cases permanently (we devote all of Chapter 7 to our people's feelings about money); and second, many of these people, the majority for sure, do not equate reduced monetary income with a lower standard of living. The explanation is simple. For the person who places a high priority on time spent with family and a low priority on acquiring things that cost money, the standard of living goes *down* when more money is earned by working longer hours and goes *up* when more free time is available. This is something of an oversimplification, of course, since some minimal level of income exists for each person, below which life is too precarious to be enjoyed. But the basic point must not be missed. For our people, standard of living usually has little or nothing to do with a level of income or consumption. Another reminder that this is indeed a "new breed."*

Besides money, some other obvious problems may be perceived as risks. Large organizations have a number of reasons for offering their employees what have come to be called fringe benefits. One is to keep them tied to the company. Tom Webb, a research consultant to the Cana-

---

*It is not difficult to understand why such people are extremely threatening to many business people and others with a strong stake in traditional ways of doing things. Our national economy is built on the necessity for constant economic growth. The fact that significant and growing numbers of people are deliberately choosing what, in conventional terms, would be described as "downward mobility" forces serious reconsideration of the very basis of our economic system and suggests a most unpredictable future. Both are bound to generate extreme anxiety in anyone whose perspective is limited to the conventional.

dian government, explains how this becomes a risk factor
for those who choose "working free":

"The main risk is really that of living in a society that is
not geared to doing what I want to do, which is to spend
part of my time earning money out in the larger society,
and part of it at home, being a sort of house-husband,
connected with my own livelihood. If you look at the structure, sure there are tax advantages to being self-employed,
but there's no disability insurance, no social security. We
have built a society which is not a very humane one."

I thought it particularly interesting that this comment
came from a person who is covered by an excellent national health insurance program. He's at least covered for
one of the very big items American free-lancers have to
pay for out of their own earnings, and it's expensive. And
very, very risky to do without. Free-lancers, not being on
payrolls, are also forced to set aside funds for tax payments and for retirement. Not exactly a risk, but certainly
an inconvenient complication that keeps many people on
the old job.

Clearly, if one chooses to step out of the usual work
pattern in our society, then risks are involved. But again,
taking risks is a normal part of life for those "working
free." More important, for most of them it's a positive,
even enjoyable, experience. Cobi Sucher:

"Well, of all the risks I took, I learned a hell of a lot more
from the *mistakes* than from what I thought was so safe and
sound and secure. But that's the only way to learn. How
else are you going to learn, except by taking risks, and
trying—sometimes over and over again? That's how I've
dealt with things. I stick my neck out, and I'm doing it
more and more. But I'm not afraid." A woman in her
fifties, living in the country a lifestyle that epitomizes frugality. Then there's ambitious young Andy Federman, an

independent film editor. Like so many other New Yorkers, he's out to make a lot of money:

"It's more unstable now, but I actually thrive on instability. I know I'm in the minority. Most people like something very stable—knowing where they're going to be next year, knowing they're going to get a thousand-dollar raise next year. I really love the idea that I could in one year double my salary—or then again, halve it, because I couldn't get the jobs."

Neither Cobi nor Andy has others to support. Obviously, having a family increases the planning and management you must do to minimize the risks. A number of our interview subjects are raising children, but their lives aren't a lot more stable and secure than the others. It's a choice people make. As Bob Marriott says, "What's the worst that can happen?"

If someone is prepared to accept the worst possibilities, that person will do a much better job handling the particular collection of problems and frustrations that goes with almost every nonstandard work style. When comtemplating a change from a traditional job to "working free," no one should ever assume that there will be fewer problems. There may even be more problems for a while, and they will, in any case, be different from those encountered in the usual work situation.

Grant Ingle earns his living as a management consultant to cooperatively managed organizations. He says he often waits a painfully long time after the work has been completed before the check arrives.

Betsy Barley spoke of a special problem of the free-lance writer, which applies pretty well to the free-lance anyS-thing: "You have to be very careful to know the people you're dealing with—what their style of working is, how much help you can really expect to get from them, other things of that kind.

"I once took a job because I needed some money to pay my taxes, and it looked like a good job. But I had two reservations about it, and both of them came to pass. The director of the program is a man that I could never get hold of when I was doing the newsletter for that organization. Never! They always told me to 'go see Bumpety-Bump,' and Bumpety-Bump was never there.

"The other problem is in the nature of nonprofit organizations. It's just a kind of attitude. They don't associate time with money, and they're not as anxious to get the job done. Therefore, they almost leave you completely alone. They don't really understand in my case that I'm not an employee, that it's not my project. They have to tell me what they want to say. I haven't lived with this thing for four years as they have."

Andy Federman talked about the pressures involved in building a reputation as a free-lancer in the big-time feature-film industry: "You're constantly having to prove to other people that you can do the job while you're working your way up. So that pressure is always on you. If you screw up, you can be sure that will be reflected the next time somebody asks that person, 'What kind of a job does he do?' If they say, 'Well, he's not that good. . . ,' that could be the kiss of death. For a lot of people it has been."

Actor Douglas Werner described a long conversation he had with his agent. Doug was faring well as far as income was concerned from appearing in commercials, but he explained, "I wanted to be contending for the feature films, the pilots, movies of the week, and the mini-series." The advice of his agent, a seasoned professional, boiled down to one essential message: "I'm sure this is a gamble, but you've got to be a gambler. If you don't want to gamble, you shouldn't be in show business."

It's not much different for free-lance writers. At some point in their careers, many writers want to break out of

doing newsletters, or ad copy, or P.R. stuff and write substantial articles for major magazines, or perhaps begin a
book. The first few rounds of writing purely on speculation—trying to find an agent who will take your work seriously, sending out proposals and manuscripts only to have
them returned over and over again, meanwhile earning
not a penny for all the work involved, with all that negative
feedback for your ego to handle—is not anyone's idea of a
stable, secure way of life. And many a good writer has
dropped by the wayside after a few months or perhaps a
few years of this kind of experience.

The next logical question is, How do people deal with
insecurity and all its problems? Essentially, it seems to
come down to personality and personal priorities. I asked
Michele Williams, "What does risk taking feel like to you?
When are you aware that you've taken a risk?"

"When it's time to pay the rent—things like that. I do
have the advantage that I can borrow money, but I feel
guilty sometimes, thinking, 'Well, I have all these loans to
pay off. Do I have the right to not be taking a 9 to 5 job?'
It's kind of like forsaking financial gain right now for long-
term advantages."

Andy Federman suggested, "People who are less worried about the instability—able to deal with it better—are
the people who make the more successful free-lancers.
Because these people are not as worried when they are
unemployed for a month. They can still enjoy themselves
and know that a good job will come along if they stick at it.
But it's not for everybody."

I happened to interview two people who were in the
midst of difficult times. Dorri Jacobs, a Manhattan writer,
consultant, and career and life-planning counselor, described a string of recent frustrations spanning several
months of effort, and then the indomitable free-lancer's
spirit came through:

"But even in the bad, bad, bad moments I was not willing to go and take a job. I could not envision working for someone else, the lack of freedom. The insecurity about money wasn't that much of an issue. What bothered me was that I just didn't know *when* things were going to get better! I wanted to *know* when they'd get better. I'm assuming that if I managed to survive for almost three years at a bad time when businesses were failing, that's a good record. And I still have money in the bank." I ran into Dorri a couple of months later and found her full of confidence, busily and enthusiastically contacting prospective publishers about her second book in process.

It's definitely not a safe, secure world when you're on your own, earning your living by your own wits and strategies; and it's very clear that a person's feelings of self-esteem make an enormous difference.

I first interviewed a woman just after she learned that the funding for her part-time job with a not-for-profit organization had run out. She actually sounded *cheerful!* And she had absolutely no idea where her next dollar might come from. This 39-year-old single woman, who has held only part-time jobs for all but nine months of her adult life, and said she has often been "reasonably comfortable" on $50 a week, shared her secret:

"Fortunately, I have a lot of *inner* security that keeps me healthy."

Then again, the next time I saw Lisa she was really down. Nobody's got it all together all the time. The important thing is that over the long haul, Lisa and all the others we are meeting in these pages are doing *what they choose* to do, risks, problems, and all.

6

The Rewards

"He is well paid that's well satisfied."
—Shakespeare
The Merchant of Venice

"The *benefits* of this kind of life? Well, here I am in the middle of the day, sitting in the sun on this porch, talking with you. . . ."

"I can very easily see myself piloting ships for the next 20 or 30 years. I'm happy in my work. I get a lot of job satisfaction from it."

"I have to be careful that I'm not enjoying myself too much. I have a tendency to go on adventures and explorations a lot, and then I ignore my bills."

Cobi Sucher, Don Metzger, Felicia Kaplan. If there is one thing the people in this book have in common it is that they are *happy*. No one is happy all the time, of course, but with a few exceptions, these are joyful, upbeat folks. It is a pleasure to be with them. The exceptions are people who are scrambling, who don't yet have their situation adequately put together, or may not know exactly what they want.

At the beginning of this book, I emphasized that I was

not writing about dropouts. The motivation of our people is not so much the limited, negative one of "getting out of the system" as it is a very positive desire to get free to do something they want very much to do. These are not professional soul searchers.* As Pat Lee said, "I consider myself a productive member of the system, but the system doesn't *own* me."

If we are to understand the real rewards that come with "working free," it is useful to return to the factor of intrinsic motivation—that powerful urge from within to do something special with your life that all of these people have. The greatest reward for them is having a chance to try out that special thing—whether it's writing, piloting ships, editing films, or becoming an independent expert on office systems or restaurants—and to discover that they can do it and make a living at it *on their own terms.*

Felicia Kaplan, who gets a real kick out of being able to do several different things well, put the matter nicely:

"I've made acquaintance with a number of free-lancers throughout Chicago, some of whom have become friends. I find them a lot more interesting than the nine-to-fivers. They have broader experiences. they have more *joie de vivre,* more enthusiasm, warmer personalities. They're not afraid to take chances, explore. Most of them are highly creative—slightly crazy, but a whole lot more fun!"

Much of therapeutic psychology in recent years by people like Abraham Maslow, Carl Rogers, and Rollo May has been directed toward helping people become more spontaneous. People who are flexible and positively oriented toward new experience are more capable of enjoying life in the present. In these terms, Felicia and the friends she

---

*By way of contrast, see the accounts of personal histories in *Breaktime: Living Without Work in a 9-to-5 World* by Bernard Lefkowitz, and *Radical Career Change* by David Krantz.

describes would have to be viewed as mentally healthy. But "happy" is just as good a word for our purposes.

As for being spontaneous, you can't beat Felicia:

"One of the most exciting things happened to me last month. Someone I met a year ago—and I had not seen her the entire year—called me out of the blue. She was giving a six-week creative writing class and asked me if I would be a guest speaker. I said, 'My God, I don't know—when?' She said, 'Oh, Monday.' This was Friday morning. I asked, 'What do you want me to talk about?' and she answered, 'Oh, just talk about how to submit writing, and where to submit it, and how to put it together.' So I just gathered all my resources and trucked out to Downers Grove, and it was great! It was my first teaching experience, and I discovered that I loved it."

This story reveals one special reward that comes with "working free," and another of the characteristics of the mentally healthy individual—personal growth. We may recall that a lack of opportunity for personal growth is one of the major reasons people give for wanting to leave bureaucratic jobs. It is therefore a goal for many of our people—and obviously something that adds greatly to their enjoyment of life.

Personal growth can mean many different things. It can be a simple experience of learning something or acquiring a new skill. Or it might be improvement in the ability to communicate with others. Or perhaps some increase in perspective—a better understanding of what is going on in the world. It may be the discovery of inner resources previously hidden. For Irma Wachtel, when she left a successful career as a computer programmer to work part-time as a consultant, it was a chance to develop some parts of her personality that had been neglected for 25 years or so.

"When I first stopped working full-time, I needed to spend a lot of time just doing whatever I pleased. Because after all those years of being under pressure—'I have to do this now, I have to that'—and never having an hour, much less a weekend free, I actually needed a couple of years off just to do whatever I pleased when I pleased to convince myself that there's nothing I really *have* to do.

"So I started doing some of the things I always wanted to do, like learning to play a musical instrument, doing a lot of folk dancing, looking at paintings, listening to music. And also reading a lot of psychology books of the kind that helped me understand myself better. That sort of makes it possible for me to be at peace with those people I may have to deal with who are sometimes a little unpleasant. They don't bother me anymore. I underwent what some people call a 'transformation,' becoming more self-actualized and generally at peace with the world. Now my only problems focus around figuring out what further advance I will put into my life and how I will enrich it."

Words on paper can't do justice to this delightful, middle-aged lady who bubbled with energy and enthusiasm as we talked. There was no doubt in my mind that the quality of her life—"standard of living," if you prefer—had improved markedly when she started trading income for more free time.

Irma blossomed through finally having some large blocks of free time, but others do it through the work itself when there are no unnecessary constraints imposed by someone else. If I didn't tell you, you might never guess that in the following exchange, Cobi Sucher was talking about her *work:*

JA: "You were saying that you seem to be able to step outside of time—that time itself just doesn't exist for you sometimes?"

Cobi: "That's right. More and more so. It's getting to be very much that way."

JA: "Is that related to your creativity? When you get into
that 'timeless' state?"

Cobi: "Yes. I think so. It's so beautiful, you know, when
everything . . . at any moment of the day I can feel the
blossoming . . . just going on and on. . . . I don't take
things all that seriously anymore. My life has become
sort of 'play.' It's serious play, but I don't take it seriously—you know what I mean? I do play with a sense of
responsibility."

Sam Love, a multitalented free-lancer, also described his
particular way of operating in the world as "play," and a
number of others came very close to the same view.

Another person who blossomed when he began "working free" was Bob Marriott. Jane said it first: "Bob is working in a way that he likes. I know he likes it. It's much more
productive for him, and he's much happier."

Bob's version: "Everything turned out to be even better
than we thought it was going to be. I'm sure that any
managerial skills I had have slipped, but I feel my *creative*
talent—whatever it was that had been shoved aside a great
deal of the time—now that I've had a chance to really find
out how good I am at it, my creativity has grown. I'm not
one of the all-time advertising and promotion geniuses,
but I am certainly better than competent, and every once
in a while I come up with something that startles me.
That's an exciting part of the business that I missed."

I don't want to leave Bob Marriott without calling attention to what Jane said: "It's much more *productive* for him."
Maybe the much-discussed decline in American productivity has some relationship to our persistently rigid work
systems. We'll have more to say on this subject in the last
chapter.

One of the obvious rewards of "working free" is just
freedom. That usually means having free time when *you*

want it or need it, and we have seen what good use Irma Wachtel makes of it. Jay Levinson's free time takes him in other directions:

"I have a much better relationship with nature. I've had so much chance to explore. I can go to a tidepool and identify 20 forms of life, whereas before I didn't even know there were 20 forms of life. I ski better now—and I skied for my college. But equipment is better, and *I have more time to do it.* I never knew about rivers, and now I've run almost all the rivers in the West, often for 20 days at a time. I never would have gotten involved with hang gliding if I didn't have the time to really check it out and get licensed to do it."

Remember, Jay is not "retired" or living on an inheritance. He works very hard—at least three days most weeks, sometimes even four. And obviously he is not living in poverty.

One of the fringe benefits to the sort of life we are discovering here is that you can avoid the busiest times for the activities that interest you. If you are a skier, you know how crowded the lift lines and the slopes are on weekends. On Mondays or Thursdays it's a whole different scene— open space!

Jay again: "The thing that amazes me, just floors me— especially in an 'enlightened' place like the Bay Area—is to go off on a hike with friends in the middle of the week and not see anybody else! I can't imagine why other people aren't doing the same thing. You can walk all day on Mount Tamalpais on a weekday and not see anybody."

I can definitely appreciate Jay's experience. I have also gotten much closer to nature and open country as a result of a decision I came to a couple of years ago. I had just put in a year working for an organization in New York City that managed to tear itself apart in the year I was there (not my fault!). It was a situation of gradually increasing tension and confusion that left me pretty well wrung out. I decided that I was going to just spend a year writing as a free-lancer. I had never had the experience of living in a rural area and was ready to give that a try. One of the benefits of free-lance writing—if you have somebody who is willing to pay for your stuff—is that you can do it almost anywhere. So I went to live in a ski chalet seven miles from Salem, New York (population 1,000), on the Vermont border—Grandma Moses country, one of the most scenically beautiful areas of the United States.

I ended up staying two years and even getting a little writing done—a start on this book, for one thing. But my time was completely my own, and I soon found myself learning the measured pace of country living. My very loose work schedule permitted cross-country skiing in the fabulous rolling hills and forests just outside my front door, catching the most delicious trout in the pond at the foot of my hill, playing a little hockey with neighbors on a frozen pond, going to country auctions, and going to town only when it was really necessary or for the Fourth of July parade. The experience of those two years of freedom in the country enriched me in a thousand ways, one of which was to give me the leisure to develop a couple of important creative projects that I'd somehow never had time for before. (Leisure as productive time is something most creative people experience and treasure.) But the major enrichment, after living in Chicago for 17 years and New York for a year, was to gain the profoundly valuable perspective of rural life and the quality of people who live in such places.

And I was free to travel when I wished. In fact, it was on a train to Syracuse that I met Vivian, who some months later became my wife.

Fringe benefits. Here's one from Doug Werner, the actor. Doug landed a small part as a soldier in the feature film *The Big Red One.* He was sent to filming sites in Tel Aviv, Jerusalem, and Dublin.

"I was there eight weeks out of a ten-week schedule, with lots of time for sightseeing. For that job I was paid $900 a week, plus overtime, travel expenses, and per diem, and there wasn't all that much to spend the money on. Over $10,000 to go halfway around the world on somebody else's money!"

"When we were in Ireland, I had about $1,000 left of the per diem, and no plans. So I said, 'I'm going to see Ireland. When the money's gone, I'll go home.' I rented a nice car and denied myself nothing for ten days. If I wanted smoked salmon, I'd get it. If I wanted champagne, I'd have champagne. It was great! I had about $150 left when I got into New York, plus a big side of smoked salmon I bought at Shannon Airport. I stayed with a friend in New York, and we ate three pounds of smoked salmon for dinner the next night. It was great!"

When you gamble in show biz, sometimes you win, and sometimes. . . . Doug's part in this particular movie ended on the cutting-room floor. No great help in getting his career in high gear.

Don Metzger not only loves his work, he's created a very nice fringe benefit for himself and for his wife. I asked Don what they usually do with the three and a half months or so he has off during the winter:

"During that time we do some traveling. We both love scuba diving—that's how we met—so we go down to the Caribbean and do some diving. Now and then we donate our time to some research outfits or donate our diving skills to assist professors on projects. We'll donate our time and talent if they will provide us with a place to stay. We've stayed in some very nice homes, had some very pleasant experiences, met some very fine people. And we've helped them. Maybe their grants aren't sufficient to cover all the needs of their project, and we supply some manpower.

"We've been to a couple of interesting conferences, and because we do live in a remote area, it's nice to go to a big city once in a while to do some big-city things. We go to New York, Washington, Toronto. . . ."

Simple *convenience* is a big payoff for many people—being able to do your shopping when you feel like it, when the stores are less crowded. Not having to worry what the boss will think if you're feeling a little low one day and just can't concentrate on work. Being able to travel on short notice. If your mother dies, you can take a couple of days off from work, right? But what if your best friend happens to be on the other side of the country, and goes into the hospital for major surgery?

Pat Lee: "When I learned that Joanne had a brain tumor, I didn't have to walk in to somebody and say, 'May I?' in order to go to California to see her. So it means working ten hours a day for a couple of extra weeks, but I didn't have to stop and think about getting permission to take the time off to go see my friend who was dying. It was *my* decision to make."

The benefits, the rewards, of "working free" come in different forms for different people. Terry Mollner spends only two hours a day trading commodities because "That's all the energy I'm willing to give to simply making money." Terry's intrinsic motivation, his goals, and the rewards he values are of a totally different sort. He happens to have a passionate interest in creating and assisting businesses that are owned and managed by the people who do the work, so he spends most of his time joyfully engaged in that mostly *unpaid* work. And while he is naturally pleased when his commodity fund is doing well for his investors—and anxious when it is not—it is clear that his great joy in life is seeing a new, employee-owned company get on its feet.

It is perhaps worth noting that very wealthy people have often turned some of their money and time toward investment in projects to benefit some aspect of society. With Terry and some others of his generation, we find altruism paramount. He's not going to wait to get rich before making his contribution to society. And Terry's modus operandi is impressive. He's very practical, very well organized, and knows exactly what he wants. I have no doubt that if Terry wanted to make a lot of money, he would, but in his view the "rewards" of life lie elsewhere: "As I got better at what I did, I realized, as I think anybody with skills and ability does, that you lack integrity if you don't use them in the best services of society."

For Terry Mollner earning a living and doing what he wants to do are closely intertwined. He has devised five principles for his life:

1. Be honest.
2. There is no choice but to be a part of the institutions you live in.
3. Make the most profit with the least amount of effort.
4. Live simply.
5. Use whatever surplus you have for the good of society.

Social do-gooders are often somber people. Not Terry. His constant ebullience, high energy, and quick, ready smile suggest a man whose rewards come with the life.

7

Money

Money was meant to be our servant. But when we depend on servants too much they gradually become our masters, because we have surrendered to them our ability to run our own lives.

—Philip Slater
Wealth Addiction

It was always a bit of a challenge to get these people to talk about money. Often when I raised the subject they would turn the conversation to something they considered more interesting. I don't think it is any special defensiveness or hesitation about money as such—it's just that for these people money does not exist as something separate from the main interests in their lives. Very few would list "making as much money as possible" as one of their major life goals.

For example, when I asked Alan Pickering how much money he needed to live comfortably, his response was:

"The work I've done to organize several little corporations was done not for money, but because I've wanted to be able to practice some skills without having to be accountable to somebody else for making mistakes. They've

72

never been money makers. What I like to do in my own life and suggest to others is to quit thinking about money, but think about a *standard of living*. That's the way I try to operate." I asked him what he meant by that. "For me, a standard of living means that I want to be able to share in those activities that provide me with the greatest amount of joy and happiness—and usually those aren't very expensive."

Alan Pickering, at age 50, was planning his twenty-first "career" change, and his plans for the future have a lot to do with his standard of living. He has acquired a five-acre wooded lot on the top of a mountain in northeastern Oklahoma, where he plans to build an earth-sheltered house utilizing solar heat and wind power as much as possible. Putting the house together will occupy his daytime hours. In the evenings he intends to manage a cable-television system. "In the move that I'm planning down to Oklahoma I expect to be able to live on a salary about two-thirds of the one I now have, but I'll maintain the same standard of living because I'm moving from a state where 12 percent of my income goes to state taxes to one that has no income tax. I'm moving from a northern climate where energy costs are very high to a climate where those costs are far lower. All of us have to find ways to be more economical with resources and use those we have more effectively."

I finally had to ask Alan again, as directly as possible, "How much money do you need to live comfortably?"

"I've put three children through college. My salary range over a work life of about 30 years has been between $10,000 and $30,000. In many cases that has been much more than I've needed—and I've known that. I've been able to save a lot of that, give a lot of it away to my children. I feel that I've been exceptionally well rewarded financially for what I've done."

The need for money and its place in life is a highly variable item among the people interviewed for this book. Sam Love told me, "As long as I know I have $300 to $400 coming in soon, I'm O.K."—and Sam lives in one of the most expensive cities in North America, Washington, D.C. And Pat Lee said, "I can make a living any place, because I can accommodate my needs to my income and my income to my needs."

Jay Levinson operates from a well-defined plan for his life: "When I moved to California from Chicago in 1971, I decided to set a goal of earning $4,000 a month working three days a week. I've been earning that consistently and achieving a balance between free time and money. Getting enough money—not a lot—but getting a lot of free time— that's more precious than money to me!"

As we will see, most of our people would consider Jay's $48,000 annual income quite a lot of money. It's all a matter of personal perspective. Jane Marriott said, "I don't think Bob and I are as goal-oriented about money as a lot of people are. We could be making about double our income if we wanted to work a little more. Or if we had decided to work that Friday, or that Saturday. We have a lot of friends who do. Both of us think of money as a means to an end, and we'd love to have it. But neither of us is directed that way, goal-oriented that way, toward the making and keeping of money, and I doubt that we will ever end up in that situation."

Michele Williams offered a theory:

"People are motivated by three things in terms of doing work. One is money, another is a desire to be helpful, and the third is a need to be creative. Money is never a real priority of mine. I'm not willing to starve, but I don't need to be wealthy. So my main priority has always been being helpful and now, coming up real quickly and maybe even passing that, is the need to be creative. I'm a great idea person, and I don't like being in environments where I can't use my imagination—boredom is one of my worst enemies."

As we have already seen, Terry Mollner's priorities fit Michelle's theory quite well, too. I was able to get him to focus briefly on the money aspect: "I very consciously chose the commodities business because it had the least risk and the highest profit, and it gave me the most free time. I wanted to make *the most money per hour* in the system. All I'm really doing is playing a game for which I get money. I have no interest in the money other than the $10,000 a year or so that I live on. The rest will go freely to support things that I think are good for society.

"I think making money is really quite silly. I've never had any respect for making money. You need money to get *things*. But I never wanted to have *things*. The only thing my father thought he owned in our house was his dresser, because my mom had all the rest of the house."

Doug Werner's response confirms part three of Michele's theory: "I'd like to be a good actor, have good parts that say something that I would like to say, with directors and other actors who take me on creative journeys. The money would come out of that. I have nothing against making a lot of money. I would like it very much, but I wouldn't want to sacrifice the other for the sake of the money. But who knows? Another few years of living on the fault line, and all that could change."

The circumstances of people's lives do change, and with those changes come changes in monetary requirements. You can't, for example, raise a family Sam Love's way: ". . . as long as I know I have $300 to $400 coming in soon. . . ." But someone who needed lots of money to put kids through college could live quite comfortably on a lot less when those expenses are over. And it's also possible for creative kids to figure out ways to finance their own education—thousands do it every year.

Given that the requirements may change many times during your life cycle, at any one time there is a certain amount of money that you need, or think you need, to be comfortable. Since aspirations of amassing great amounts of money are not, with one or two exceptions, characteristic of our people, I chose to concentrate on the perceived *need* and on what the money is needed for.

I asked Pat Lee, "What is your absolute, rock-bottom requirement for money per month?"

"My rent is too high. That takes over $350 a month. I have a loan that I took out to pay for my typewriter—that's $87 a month. And my phone bill runs upwards of $50. Utilities are another $30. Charge accounts are maybe another $100 plus. I guess I need $1,000 a month to live on, and it's a struggle sometimes. Some of that stuff of course is tax deductible—I don't know what my taxes are going to be at the end of the year. Oh, and medical insurance has got to cost me around $40 a month.

"None of this allows for stuff like trips to the dentist— and my major medical has a $500 deductible on it, which really stinks. I've got to look around for better medical insurance. . . ."

It is interesting that when I asked for a monthly figure it took a while for Pat to come up with it. She didn't say right off, "At least $1,000 a month." I found this to be quite a common pattern with these people. They tend to live very much in the present. They would have a pretty good fix on their financial situation at the moment, but it was rare when one of them could give an immediate answer to the monthly budget question.

The answer I got from Felicia Kaplan, for example, was

in dramatic contrast to Jay Levinson's carefully planned $4,000 a month—in more than one way!

JA: "What's a comfortable income for you? What amount of money enables you to pay your bills and have enough left over for whatever else you need?"

Felicia: "I have no idea. It's kind of foot to mouth—what do they call it? Hand to mouth. When things get tough or tense or tight, I know that I've got to do something in a hurry. I tend to do very well under pressure—like around the 20th of the month, if I need several hundred dollars I've been very quick to find it somehow. Right now I'm a little bit more careful about having a steady flow coming in—I'm probably the farthest ahead right now than I've been in a long time, partially because of an error I made in figuring my checking account. I forgot to enter a deposit several months ago and it showed up."

JA: "What does a lot more ahead mean? Several hundred, a couple hundred?"

Felicia: "Yes. You know I've never been too good on budgeting despite the frugality. I'm very good at maneuvering on a small amount of money. Like what I've been doing the last year or so is carrying only $3 a day on me and that has to cover lunch and transportation. That's all I take. Because I know if I take $10, I'll spend $10. If I take $5 I'll spend $5. If I take $3, that's all I have and I have to make the most of it. My bills are not tremendous. Even in times when I didn't work for three or four weeks at a stretch, when I didn't have any money coming in at all, I always managed to pay the rent. I couldn't figure out sometimes where it actually came from. I have been known to exist on $10 for 10 days. I have been known to have soup for 5 days straight. I always ate once a day. People tend to give me

things a lot. People are always giving me things. I don't
ask—people just offer. It's really amazing. So I asked
some people, 'What is it?' And they said, 'Well, we don't
feel sorry for you, we just like you.' "

Felicia Kaplan is the person who, among so many other
things, runs workshops on the topic of "frugal living." She
would appreciate Cobi Sucher:

JA: "What about money? How much do you need to survive a year?"

Cobi: "Well, up until last year I was living on about $2,000
a year. But now the costs have gone up, you know, heat
and everything else. I bought my house for $2,600. It
was a gas station then."

JA: "What's your need for annual income now that costs
have gone up?"

Cobi: "Probably close to $4,000 by now."

JA: "At that level of income do you feel you are just barely
surviving, or are you comfortable, or what?"

Cobi: "That's all up to the individual. I think I'm doing
great. Other people would object to the way I live."

JA: "But you don't feel that you are under financial pressure?

Cobi: "No, but you see things are a little more complicated
than that in a way. Because my husband died in '64, and
he left a little money in the bank at the time. I have
always made it grow, and I know I can fall back on that
little bit of capital. Sometimes when I really need money,
I can withdraw the interest, but I've never touched the
capital. That's one thing I'll never do. Isn't that strange?
That's my old Dutch ways."

JA: "What about health insurance or any other insurance?"

Cobi: "I don't have health insurance at all. I have to have insurance on my car, so I have the *minimum*. No life insurance. I don't believe in it. If you have health insurance, you'll get sick. It's like sickness insurance. I figure now, see, I have my little bit of capital in the bank, so if I ever really get sick . . . you know if I can save $300 or more a year on health insurance, you know what I mean, I just have it saved for myself instead of paying it to the health-insurance people."

JA: "How do you manage to live on $2,000 or $4,000 a year?"

Cobi: "Well, first of all . . . I don't know. I've never even thought about that. You rarely buy anything *new*. You just don't do that. Before you consider buying anything that's new, always consider secondhand, and usually you can find it."

JA: "Do you usually have to go outside of South Haven to find things?"

Cobi: "No. I'm better off not going out of South Haven. I'm better off staying right here and watching my own little town, and generally it seems whatever I need comes my way. Because I hardly ever study the advertisements or anything. I do go to a lot of rummage sales and church sales. I must admit, though, I did buy a new wood stove. But the other thing is that my living expenses are not very high. Like my telephone is a party line, and I keep that bill down to a minimum. And I'm always watching when I use hot water not to let it run. Little things like that. And this sounds kind of petty, maybe, but it does make a difference. I only take a bath once a week. I think that's all I need. I'm not into this heavy cleaning trip, either. I don't have a washer and I don't have a drier. I bought enough underwear to last me for two, three weeks, right? So I wear clean underpants every day. I'll do that. So I don't have to wash for two or three weeks. So I just take the whole kit and caboodle and just put it in the car and go to the laundromat. And it costs me a dollar to run the great big machine all at once. And I don't use the drier. I hang the stuff on the line outside, which I prefer, you know. I like to be outdoors in the wind and feel the laundry flapping around, and just be out there where the birds are singing. I like it. I really like it."

JA: "Do you do that even in the winter?"

Cobi: "Sure, on nice sunny days you're out in the snow there, tramping around, hanging out the laundry . . . sometimes it freezes, but who cares? Oh, on a very heavy, rainy day I'd use the drier maybe, but I resent having to use a drier. I really do. It's just a basic feeling that I have, and I resent it.

"Other ways you can save? I don't know . . . just don't buy a hell of a lot of stuff. Even food, you know, I buy just little bits. Of course I ride my bike every day, right, so I can only take little bits. I can't carry more than about $20 worth of groceries. Sometimes I'll skip a lot of meals. I'm usually too busy to eat anyway."

JA: "Your work is so good that you could go into a major city and turn this into a highly profitable business. Would you ever do that?"

Cobi: "I think that would ruin it. I think it would ruin the whole thing."

JA: "Why?"

Cobi: "I don't want to work that hard, John. It's plain and simple as that. I don't want to work that hard. I think if I went into the city, there would be this big overhead, right? There'd be $600-a-month rent to pay. And I'd have to go like crazy, and get seamstresses to work for me. I'd go nuts! I like it *this way.* I can sit on the porch here and talk to you, instead of running around like crazy. And I'm making a living. I'm not making *money.* That's the point, see? I don't want to spend all that

money, and I don't want to make all that money. I just
want to live. And I'm just too lazy—to tell you the
truth—to go into big business. I don't want it."

JA: "You went to Holland, so you needed more than just a
little bit of money. What do you do when you need
money for something special?"

Cobi: "My money in the bank accumulates interest, and I
feel free to draw on the interest. So I do have that back
of me."

JA: "Could you imagine living the way you do without that
money in the bank? What does it mean to have that
there? It seems like an important factor."

Cobi: "Well, I think the money that I have in the bank gives
me freedom. Yes. But you know the word 'freedom' can
be misinterpreted in so many ways . . . I don't know . . .
I've just developed a lifestyle that can only be the way it
is. There is no question that I'd say, well if I didn't have
that money, what would I be doing? I'd be doing something else, but I don't know what. Except that I know
that anytime that I'm put into bondage, any kind of
structure, I get very upset. Always have."

"Poverty" begins to look a little different, doesn't it?
Felicia and Cobi are relaxed, happy people. You don't get
any feeling at all of either of them being under pressure.
But of course both of these women are exceptional in their
skills at low-cost living, and most people with alternative
work arrangements will never need to get by on $4,000 a
year. I have given these accounts some space here because
I feel it is important for people to see that a drastic reduction in one's income for a while does not mean starvation.
In my own case, the first time I left the standard job scene
I was quickly amazed at how little money I was spending,
whereas before it was gas to get back and forth to work,
clothes, cleaning, a felt need for "entertainment" a couple

of nights a week to get my mind off the job stuff—all of the costs that go with holding down a regular job. It's an interesting exercise for anyone contemplating "working free" to draw up a list of typical monthly expenses that are directly connected with the present job.

Lest we think that frugality is the only way to go, Dick Wakefield was, when I interviewed him, planning a sort of semiretirement at age 60 after many years of working in government and in corporate jobs. His annual income has been around $45,000, and now he will have a pension bringing in $17,000. Dick says, "That will take care of two days a week that I can use to do what I want, and I am currently negotiating for a part-time job for the three other days of the week, which will provide the rest of the $45,000." Of course, he won't necessarily do this weekly sort of routine, which means that sometimes he may work full-time at his part-time job for a couple of weeks, then have a week free for his other interests. And some of these other interests may turn into income opportunities as well. Among other things, Dick's got three houses to support, and the cost of living in Washington, D.C., where he lives most of the time, is very high.

Bob and Jane Marriott, both working somewhat less than full-time, have found their monthly income quite variable—"We have months when we make $10,000 and months when we make $1,000"—but their annual income has been increasing steadily, from $25,000 just three years earlier to around $60,000 at the time of the interview. Bob shares in paying college expenses for his daughter and sends her an allowance, but they have no other unusual expenses.

There is no doubt that having a good income can increase one's freedom. In the case of the Marriotts it shows up in their attitude toward the financial side of their work.

"We're not the only company that does this kind of

work. Bigger companies do it, but bigger companies tend to be more expensive than we are. We can afford to work for somebody who couldn't afford to hire some of the big guys in the business. I mean, some consultants don't even want to talk about a project if it's not worth $25,000 or up. But we can afford to work for an individual restaurant, for example. It's not the most profitable part of our business, and if we really added up the hours we've put in on some of those businesses, it would barely be profitable. But we can afford to do that sometimes just for the fun of it—if there is somebody we really like, and we like the kind of restaurant he has. We have a great guy who runs a restaurant in Phoenix. He's a nut. We didn't make any money working for 'Crazy Ed,' but we had such a good time . . . some of the ideas we came up with . . . well, there were no limits . . . the nuttier it was, the better he liked it!"

A person's attitudes toward money are always closely related to other values and priorities. Mike Pavilon said, "I have high ambitions around money. In order to live the way I want to live now I need to make about $25,000 a year. What do I want? I want to make a hundred grand a year."

With his various projects, Mike is already putting together pretty full days. My guess is that with his financial goal, work is gradually going to take up more and more of his life. It will be interesting to see. I asked him why he wanted so much money.

"I want some power and influence. Not only do I want to have the influence and enjoy people personally, but I would like to have some political and economic influence in the city of Chicago."

Andy Federman appears very likely to earn the level of income Mike Pavilon aspires to. This 23-year-old film sound editor is already well on his way. One advantage to free-lancing in the entertainment industry is that the stan-

dard pay levels are usually set by unions, which also set
important provisions for overtime in a business where
much of the work gets done well beyond a normal eight-
hour day. Andy explained:

"First of all, in my field you end up working an enormous amount of overtime. The sound is the last thing
that's done, so they give it the shortest amount of time
because of the enormous cost. You know, if somebody
invests $10 million in a film, they're paying out just in
interest rates per day more than they're paying their
editors. So however many editors they can bring on, and
however much time they can work them, that's how much
they will. So there's a possibility of earning enormous
amounts of overtime."

We'll see in the next chapter what that sort of work
schedule actually looks like. When I talked with Andy he
had been earning about $300 a week as a studio staff per-
son. He expected that the rate would more than double as
a free-lancer. Andy's considered an exceptionally competent sound editor, and as his reputation grows from giving
high-quality work to producers, the price he can charge
for his work will also go up. He made an amusing comment about his earning potential:

"My mom always wanted me to be a lawyer or a doctor.
A friend of mine, my age, will soon be getting out of law
school. One time I figured out that, at a good-paying law
job, over the course of his life he will not earn as much
money as I will. He'll have a more stable job, but the
financial prospects for mine will be greater. My mom was
proud of that."

Andy takes the creative side of his work very seriously,
and even though he also has some monetary ambitions,
they're secondary. And like so many of the others we've
met in these pages, he enjoys one of the major fringe
benefits of "working free":

"There are a lot of other benefits besides the money. When you work 80 hours a week for a period of, say, two months, you've essentially put in four months' worth of work at a regular job. So, if you were to take the next two months off, you would have put in the same number of hours as somebody who works 40 hours a week, but you would have probably got paid three times the amount because of the overtime pay rates."

Francine Rizzo has extraordinary skills in the lucrative field of information processing, and she's been a whiz at making money since age nine. She was so captivated by the possibilities for making money that she dropped out of high school to take a part-time job with a market research firm. By age 22 she was a supervisor in another market research firm with 50 people working for her. With this background, I had no trouble accepting her statement that now, at age 36, "I could make a lot of money. . . ." The other end of that sentence was, "but that is not my primary motivation." Guess what was?

"My primary motivaton is to have my freedom most of the time and work when I want to and to live and to do whatever I want to do. I don't want to have a Rolls-Royce, and I don't want to go around the world three times a year, so my needs are basically modest."

Some people who acquire the knack of making a lot of money seem to get compulsive about it and end up devoting their whole lives to the money-making trip. But others who clearly have the aptitude and knowledge for making money at some point decide that other things are more important. Francine reached that point very early in her life. Rowlie Sylvester had, over the years, invented and patented a number of tools and devices used in tire making, and owned several successful manufacturing companies. At age 45 he decided he wanted to spend his time and energy in other ways, and by 50 he had sold off all his

businesses and moved from a big house in South Bend to a
log cabin in the woods near South Haven. He travels a lot,
including time on the Great Lakes in a roomy old boat that
he salvaged and renovated. Rowlie had been out of the
business world (except for keeping a good eye on his investments) for 11 years when we talked. Here's what he
had to say about money:

"I used to say that a good way to be independent was to
live cheap and travel light. I don't have very high overhead. I don't spend money lavishly. I don't spend much at
all, actually. I might start spending a little more now.
There's a different kind of inflation. You might call it
'negative inflation.' That is, man, you get older, you don't
need that money around forever. So, what's the point?

"I think there is something about money that is over-
looked sometimes, and that is that it's really important to
know how to handle it—to make it work for you rather
than you working for the money. And rather than having
a whole lot of time payments on cars and refrigerators and
TV sets, and other things . . . if you've got money that you
have earning interest or bringing in some rents or divi-
dends, or you can buy and sell things—maybe buy a house
and fix it up and sell it. That's a lot different from paying
interest on a house.

"The money system isn't so hard to figure out. I had to
do that. I had to take what resources I had and learn about
investments. To me, that's just accepting the economy that
exists and making it work for you rather than being the
victim of the economy. It exists. It's out there. I don't have
anything against it."

Money is, of course, supposed to be some kind of an
indicator of value, and I am impressed by Rowlie Sylvester's tendency to increase the value of things others would
overlook, instead of collecting expensive possessions. He
salvaged and renovated that old boat so he could *use* it, not

as a status symbol. He turned an old waterfront shack into a marina. And he has spent a lot of time these past few years hunting down all sorts of old boats and then restoring them for his Great Lakes Maritime Museum. And while none of these things put any significant amount of money in his pocket, they certainly represent valuable contributions to the quality of his life as well as to that of his community. And when Rowlie took Vivian and Molly and me out on his boat to watch the "Venetian Night" festivities at the Chicago lakefront, the quality of our lives was way up there for a while, thanks to his creativity and generosity.

It's clear that whether you're working at a standard job or "working free," the place of money in your life really has a lot to do with *attitudes*. Philip Slater's *Wealth Addiction* describes one set of attitudes. There's another book, by Michael Phillips, called *The Seven Laws of Money,* which many people working on their own terms swear by. Given the conditioning around money that most of us are subjected to, I should not be surprised if the accounts in this chapter still leave some readers a little nervous and suspicious. Reading Slater and Phillips should help to fill in the blanks, and overcome some of that old conditioning. More important, it may help you answer Slater's key question: "Do you rule money or does money rule you?"

8

Managing Time

I may not work for a number of days, even a number of weeks, and then suddenly I'll become very busy. I will work 14 hours a day or 10 hours a day over a period of time, and then I can relax again. There's an ebb and flow in my work. It's a great thing. I can get a deadline that will seem tight to the client, but I know from my experience that I can mess around with the time on it according to what's more beneficial to me in my personal life. That's one of the reasons I have this situation.

—Francine Rizzo

We found in Chapter 3 that a major reason people give for leaving 9 to 5 jobs is to have more control over the use of their time. And that may mean hours of the day, days of the week, or weeks of the year. Some people feel that they work best at certain times of the day and don't want to be forced to perform during their "down" times. Others feel that life is out of balance without a three-day weekend every week. Others want large blocks of time off from work for other pursuits—travel, community activities, writing a book, being with family.

But in order to enjoy this sort of freedom, a person must

88

have enough self-discipline to work when it's time to work. A person's ability to manage and make the best use of time is clearly a key factor in success at "working free." Raymond Mungo, in his engaging book, *Cosmic Profit: How to Earn Money Without Doing Time,* observes, "You know you've grown up when you finally learn to budget your time."

Most of us have a feeling that self-discipline is something acquired through great pain and sacrifice. Sometimes that's the way it develops, but I sensed as I talked with all of these people that self-discipline evolved gracefully for most of them. As people found that they could actually earn a living doing exactly what they wanted to do, their energy for and attention to the task at hand increased, and potential distractions exerted less and less power. After all, if you can have fun doing your work, why waste your time on something else?

It's not always that simple, of course. Most of us know something about the psychological games we play with ourselves from time to time, and those inner tricksters have prevented many potentially creative people from actually producing anything when they finally had the free time to do it. I remember once hearing about a college professor who got a long-desired year off with full pay at the very comfortable and peaceful Center for Advanced Study in the Behavioral Sciences in Palo Alto, California. Many a fine book and hundreds of scholarly articles have been written in that lovely spot. But this man, finally faced with a year of free time—no classes, no students to advise, no committee meetings—spent the first few days just sitting, staring off into space . . . and the next few days . . . and. . . . At the end of his sabbatical year he had played a lot of volleyball and darts, becoming quite good at both, and enjoyed many wonderfully stimulating conversations with his colleagues, and had not written one page.

This true story suggests several possibilities. One is that this is a person who can be productive only when someone else provides the structure, the demands, the schedule. Another possibility is that he did not have a strong enough intrinsic motivation about any particular project to keep the distractions at bay. Another is that he may very well have needed and deserved a good rest. Or he may have had serious psychological problems that he could remain unaware of as long as he was in a structured work pattern imposed by someone else, but which came to the fore when he had time to face himself.

A whole book could be written on the subject of self-discipline and how to achieve it. There are many paths. We'll have more to say on that subject in Chapter 12— some specific suggestions to help you avoid the volleyball syndrome.

Once you step out of the traditional 9 to 5 routines, the possibilities are unlimited. The total amount of time a person works over the course of a year may be related in a fairly direct way to the amount of money that person perceives a need for. But on the other hand, there are ways of working in which the relationship of hours or days worked to income is not all that clear. For example, every competent commission salesman with a few years of experience can tell of times when he worked long, hard days for perhaps months with very little financial return, and perhaps another time when a third of his annual income developed out of two weeks of effort. Time is not necessarily money. Badly used time is absolutely not.

And time takes on different meanings to different people. Various people have proudly said to me, "My work is an alternative to 9 to 5. I work from 7 A.M. until 7 P.M. most days, including weekends." Sam Love told me several years ago, "I work for money about three months out of the year. I need the rest of the time free to think and do a little writing." But Sam's work time increased dramatically after he launched a new business. Cobi Sucher told me, "I work pretty much when I feel like it." And Ken Dagdigian, who recently added a West Coast office to his small, Chicago-based educational publishing business, remarked, "People in California have a very different attitude toward work time. Out there, working hard is when you play tennis only one afternoon a week." Then there's Californian Bob Marriott, who plays tennis almost every afternoon. He's usually on the court by 2 o'clock. But then Bob typically starts his workday at 5:30 A.M.

Let's take a look at the way a couple of people in the entertainment industry manage their time. The entertainment industry, with the exception of some network or studio executives and staff, is largely composed of freelancers. And it is worth noting that entertainment has been one of the major growth industries of the past couple of decades. What with television (including commercials), movies, the great recent blossoming of live music, theater, and dance performances all over the country, the recording industry, and professional sports, a whole lot of people are earning a living—or at least some part of a living—as actors, dancers, musicians, agents, road managers, film editors, and directors. Two of those people are actor Doug Werner and film sound editor Andy Federman.

It seems Doug Werner never stops working. In the 4 years he has been in the trade since his graduation from the drama school at the University of Southern California, he has done quite a few TV commercials, has had small roles in a couple of TV movies, was a regular on the TV soap opera "Edge of Night" for a year, and spent a couple of months working on a major feature film. As this is written, he is in Chile filming another commercial.

I asked Doug about his time allocations with regard to

TV commercials. It turns out most of it is interviews and preparations, which may or may not pay off with a job.

"I go on the average of one or two interviews a week. I'd say between 15 and 20 minutes to get there, another half-hour to an hour waiting in line, then going in and doing the interview, then another 15 to 20 minutes to get home. Let's say an hour and a half to two hours for the first interview. Then sometimes a callback, which is another two hours, then maybe another callback, which is another one to two hours."

For every hour of interview time, there are also some hours of preparation:

"Sometimes you have to have the right 'look' when you go in there. You have to call your agent to find out if they're looking for the lumberjack type, the young executive type, a young husband. You want to look the part as much as you can to give them the opportunity to see you in that role.

"And then memorization of the lines. If it's a callback, you want to have it pretty well memorized so you can get off the page. Then, if you get the part, there are a couple of days when you spend an hour or two for wardrobe fittings to figure out what you're going to wear. For the actual commercial shooting you better count on a whole day—6:30 or 7:00 in the morning until 7:00 or so at night, plus travel time to and from. Generally they're pretty fast on commercials because they're expensive. So you're generally done in 12 hours."

The actor's life is one in which the relationship between expenditure of time and income is hard to pin down, at least during the career-building stage. Most actors who have not yet made it big are constantly refining their skills, working with voice teachers, doing bodywork, attending classes or workshops. Doug Werner described the work involved in training himself for possible dramatic roles in films or plays:

"If you consider the time I spend in class, the time I spend going to auditions, the time I spend in pursuing work just in terms of talking to people, making rounds . . . any day that goes by that I don't do at least one or two things—like go to class, or go to an audition, or talk to my agent, or go read some plays, rehearse a scene for acting class—I feel I'm really wasting time. It eats away at me. I feel heavy guilt."

I asked him what he felt guilty about.

"I'm guilty because I'm not working. Maybe I'm doing something wrong. I just lose my self-esteem when I see other people working and I'm not. It's jealousy and bitterness and feelings like that, which just drive you down instead of keeping you up."

Of course almost everyone who has ever had to go out and look for a job knows those feelings. But free-lancers, no matter what kind of skills they have, are *always* at least partly involved in looking for an assignment and preparing themselves for whatever opportunities may turn up. It's part of the life.

Andy Federman seems to have a lot of free time, but when he works, he *works!*

"I worked on a feature film, for example, and worked on the average about 80 hours a week. This was a major feature under Warner Brothers. I would say that is not abnormal, especially toward the end, when I was working even longer hours! A couple of time I've said to myself: 'They could pay me a thousand dollars an hour right now, but it wouldn't be worth it in exchange for the sleep I need.'"

There is a handsome monetary payoff for this high-pressure work, but if one is going to survive physically, intense periods of work must be balanced out with blocks of free time to recuperate. Federman says it is not unusual to work for two or three months and then take off a couple of months before starting the next job. "Unemployment" has a distinctly different meaning in this context!

Andy Federman's is not the only job where the intensity of the work, or the pressure, or the sheer irregularity of a normal work schedule make a large block of time off on a regular basis a *necessity* for preserving health and emotional stability. Mike Galbraith made this point with regard to the work pressures of a chef.

Don Metzger earns his living piloting ships through the St. Lawrence Seaway. His description of the demands of the job makes his annual, long winter vacation seem more than just a nice fringe benefit:

"I'm self-employed as a pilot of salt-water ships— foreign ships—that enter the St. Lawrence-Lake Ontario portion of the seaway system. I pilot the ships to their various ports, through locks and up and down the river, across the lake and into the harbors—shipping, anchoring, and piloting. I act as a guide to the ship's master. The captain of the ship is coming into a place that maybe he has never been to before, with language barriers, and he doesn't know the regulations. I get on board and basically handle the ship for him in the brief time that he's in the seaway system.

"Since ships work 24 hours a day, pilots have to work 24 hours a day. The seaway is frozen with ice for about three and a half months out of the year, so for that time I'm essentially unemployed—my vacation break. That's a time block to do whatever I want. It's also a mental-health time, because during the summer, from the middle of April or May to the middle of December, I'm working a very hectic kind of schedule. I only get six days off out of the month. The rest of the days I'm working steadily—when I say days, I mean 24-hour days. I've got to be handling ships during the night just as much as I'm handling them during the day, so I just sort of catch rest when I can. When there's a shipping lull you rest.

"But you're still on standby. You never know when the fog is going to lift, or when the *Paul Jones* is going to fix its engine and get under way and get into your district so you can board it and take it to wherever it is going. So even when you're not working for one or two days, you're still on a standby basis. Many times I have to carry a telephone pager when I go to the beach or to a show or out to dinner, because I never know what might happen. So it's a very crazy schedule, or nonschedule, whatever you call it. It can upset your biological clock if you let it."

I asked Don Metzger how he deals with that biological clock problem:

"I try to set aside periods of time during the day or night for deep relaxation—a kind of yoga—and I try to keep myself in good physical shape by jogging or swimming whenever I can. I also try to take naps whenever the opportunity allows."

Joan Clebus is a Toronto mother of two who has worked at several different part-time jobs, sometimes more than one at a time. One of her favorites is working for the Toronto Convention Bureau, helping out in various ways at whatever conventions come into the city from time to time. When we talked, she was handling the information booth in the main concourse of the "First World Congress on the Future" at the Harbor Castle Hilton. Joan's description of the demands of this sort of work sounded a little like Don's. "Hours and days are quite variable. It could be morning, afternoon, or crazy hours like 7 A.M. till 10 P.M." She explained that she was virtually on call at any time for these jobs, often on short notice, and added, "You have to be flexible—able to manage the homelife." Her relaxed, pleasant manner made it clear that she was managing all this quite comfortably while raising two teenagers.

The demanding work schedules that Andy and Don and Joan describe are, of course, set by someone else. Don's options are quite limited, but Andy could choose to take on fewer film jobs, and Joan could work fewer conventions, so there is at least that degree of freedom. The ultimate freedom comes with being your own boss, creating your own work. And work schedules are chosen rather than imposed.

Terry Mollner talked about how he schedules that part of the day he devotes to earning money: "It's wonderful, because I can get up in the morning and do my work in about an hour—if need be I can do it in 20 minutes—I chart in the prices of all the commodities I'm in, take a look at where the system says I should go, and simply change the stops. And that's it. I can simply forget about it the rest of the day. I take two hours to do it because I like it, and I like to check everything as the market opens. So the rest is free time."

Cobi Sucher doesn't make any real distinction between work time and free time:

"I get up around 7 or 8 in the morning, have a cup of tea. I begin to pick up energy, and the first thing I do is get on my bicycle. I love it. I get into town. I usually pick up a bite to eat in town, because breakfast is fairly cheap. I pick up my shopping and come home, and I'm usually full of energy by then. Ten miles of bike riding a day, seven days a week—I do it about eight months out of the year.

"Then sometimes I just feel like sitting and reading a book. I come home from the bike ride and I just sit a little bit, just read a book and think about what I'm going to do next—what I would like to do next. There's always a sewing job, some order waiting to get done. And I'm working on this wedding outfit—that's a biggie. It'll bring in about

$200. So I'll work on it about ten days. And sometimes I just sit with absolutely nothing . . . almost with a certain sort of stage fright.

"With the wedding dress, it must have been three days that I just sat. I'd read for half an hour . . . this doesn't work . . . do I start the dress? No, I just sit there and look at it and look at it. Couldn't decide, because it was dangerous. You know, I had this beautiful silk—it was awfully expensive material. I had no pattern. I had to just cut it, so finally I said, 'Now you *have* to do it, you *have* to do it.' So I put a sheet on the kitchen floor, crawled around on my hands and knees, and *I cut it!* Then I started feeling good. Then I picked up energy, and I just worked on it *all the time*.

"And then once in a while something happens in the morning, or I meet someone in town, and my whole day will be completely different from the way I planned it. And who cares. Like today, you wanted to do this interview. I say, 'All right, I was going to go home and put the buttons on the shirt, but I guess I won't. I'll do it later.'

"I don't consider time either free time or working time. It's *my* time. It's my now-living time."

Of course, even when you are creating your own work, and not meeting some client's or employer's schedule, other factors will require special kinds of time management. A family, for example.

Jessica Lipnack and Jeffrey Stamps were in the process of writing a book on "networking" when I interviewed them. Having two small children in the house, which is also where they work, complicates things a bit:

"We have someone who comes to take care of the children from 9 to 5. That's the basic time slot when we're both free. And then we use the times around that to free up each other. So on weekends one of us will work, and the other will take care of the kids.

"Our biggest situational issue is around child care, be-

cause that's been the major constraint. We wouldn't nor-
mally work 9 to 5. But that's something that baby-sitters
can relate to. [A baby was crying in the background.]
There are a lot of influences . . . I mean, I feel like the
world forces you into a lot of things that you wouldn't
necessarily do unless you had to. In other words, you can't
get a baby-sitter who will come from 3 until 9. It's a lot
easier to get somebody who will work 9 to 5. Mostly, we're
working until about 9 or 10 at night, and just trading off
on the other stuff that has to be done."

I asked if they ever take some time off:

"I think we're both relatively driven, sometimes to a bad
degree. We don't know how to take as many rests as we
should. We just took ten days off. We finished nine chapters of the book and sent them in, and took ten days off.
But that was the first break we've had in a long time. I
think we both tend to work the way a lot of artists work,
which is that you just keep working until you complete
your project. If you don't, then you lose the momentum.
It's different from piecemeal kind of work that you can
pick up and put down."

Donald Michael is quite a successful social scientist who
recently made a transition from a professorship at the
University of Michigan to a life of free-lance writing and
consulting in California. His description of a typical daily
and weekly schedule was quite detailed:

"The first part of the day—I get up early, 5:30, 6:00—
that's if I'm in good spirits. If I'm depressed or struggling
with emotional matters, I find I sleep longer. But generally
speaking I'm up early. I love being up early. The first part
of the day goes into exercise: jogging alternating with yoga
and some meditation and that kind of activity. The first
part of the day also goes to making phone calls to the East
Coast, because before 8:00 A.M. they're a lot cheaper. I
always have been a great phone user, and I find now the

phone is even a much more important part of my life. I've always used it creatively.

"My writing time is usually in the morning because that's when I'm more 'writeable.' I'm more clear-headed and incisive. If I'm doing any really tough reading, I'm more likely to do it then, though I find I can do some of that in the evening. I will try to schedule my appointments in the afternoons, because that way writing time and thinking time aren't interfered with. I need the extra stimulus of people in the afternoon because that's when my metabolism tends to be on the slow side."

"Once or twice a week I may well be at SRI, one of the places I do part-time work now. Or, from time to time I may have appointments with other clients or other consultants that I'm working with. I try to avoid lunch, and if I'm working at home I skip it. But lunch is a good time to meet with people, and I often use it for that purpose.

"Evenings are focused around reading or maybe socializing dinners. They may be out or at home. I do my own cooking."

"I find that my days of the week are not, for the most part, structured with work on the first five days, then doing other things on Saturday or Sunday. I may just as well work hard all through Saturday evening and be off on social or nonwork activities on Tuesday evening. It just depends on how it goes. One of the things that has been a delight to me has been to find out that I could break loose from that, and not feel oppressed or left out if I were working on a Saturday night rather than being out with people, that kind of thing. That's been a nice release from the old pattern."

When I heard this last part, it reminded me of my own experience with the newness of flexible free time the first time I left a regular job after many years of routines to live my life on my own terms.

I was living in Chicago at the time. It was late spring and the weather was getting nicer each day. I had always enjoyed riding my bike along the lakefront for miles or going to the beach a few blocks from my house. With my new freedom I found myself at the lakefront for long periods every time the weather was nice. It was weeks before it finally dawned on me that I didn't need to be compulsive about enjoying myself. There would be plenty of time for it. Then I discovered that I could stay indoors and get some work done even though it was a beautiful day outside, and not resent it.

I had another revelation in a favorite hangout listening to some superb Chicago blues on a Wednesday night only days after I had left the job for good. At one point I looked at my watch. It was 11:30 and I started getting uptight about having to leave. Then it suddenly dawned on me that, even though it was a weeknight, I didn't have to be anywhere the next morning! What a liberation *that* was! I bought another round of drinks for my friends in celebration, and stayed till 2:00 A.M., closing time. As usual, the music just kept getting better and better the later it got. A week later I left for ten days in the Virgin Islands. I could just as well have stayed there longer if I'd wanted to. . . .

Free-lance writing tends to be one of the lonelier pursuits. The demand to sit alone all day and be creative is a difficult one. Hence the well-known problem of "writer's block"—and the hundreds of strategies writers have devised for preventing or overcoming it.

Like most free-lance writers, Betsy Barley has times when the work goes well, and other times when she can't seem to maintain the essential rhythm of daily work. She described what this feels like:

"There is no such thing as a typical work day or week. I think if I could get myself into a rhythm of more writing time . . . I tend to be at everybody's beck and call. I think if

I could actually map out four days a week that I would be at my typewriter and not leave it, and then spend a day uptown, that would work. As it is I just try to schedule a bunch of things uptown at the same time. I think I just need more discipline to make myself actually sit down and do the writing."

Betsy suggested at this point that the unstructured aspect of free-lancing can lead to a lot of distractions. "I think I could be real proud of myself if I beat those distractions, but I haven't quite done it yet." I reminded her that she was earning over $15,000 a year without perfect self-discipline.

"Yes. I get things done. Only very rarely do I fail to meet a deadline . . . except this one time. I think I got tired and I was real mad. I said, 'OK, if I can't get hold of you, you get hold of me!' Then I went off traveling for two months. It did work. We are now finishing up real fast."

I have known Betsy for a long time. Over the past couple of years she has been working off and on at writing an interesting book of her own. It is my impression that she is more easily distracted when she actually has free time to devote on her own book than when she is free-lancing a project for someone else. I know for sure that happens to me. Maybe some of us have particular difficulty doing what is good for ourselves—often just the thing that will bring us the greatest satisfaction and freedom!

9

Work and the Rest of Your Life

Do we work to live or live to work?
—Max Weber

The big question when we were children was, "What do you want to be when you grow up?" No one ever thought to ask, *"What sort of a life do you want to be living when you grow up?"*

At the time, the right question was being asked, because until the last 10 or 15 years, most people looked for and found identity in the *work* they did. And the kinds of work one's parents did could be safely predicted as possible career fields for young people facing the future. There was a reassuring sense of security and stability about this scheme of things. In 1955 a teenage girl could decide that she would be a housewife and mother; or perhaps a teacher, nurse, or airline stewardess for a few years before she settled into that role. (There was never anything in the plan beyond the housewife-mother stage.) Similarly, a boy could say with confidence, "I am going to be a doctor"—or a coach, or an engineer; and after the standard number of years in educational institutions, he could reasonably expect to spend the next 40 years or so earning a living (and

102

supporting a family) at his chosen craft. He also expected to have a lot of free time for fishing and trips to Europe when he reached the "golden age" of retirement at 65.

If there is a significant audience for this book, it is mostly because the traditional life plan no longer makes any sense for large numbers of people. Everything in the standard formula has changed. And some degree of anxiety is a normal response when one's well-nurtured expectations, cultivated and reinforced over many years, lose their validity.

This is not to suggest that a young person should not be thinking seriously about the kind of work he or she will do as an adult. I do think, however, that plans about work and earning a living should be part of a larger context, a more encompassing set of considerations. Social changes occur at a rapid rate, and an intelligent youngster, along with parents and guidance counselors, will do well to look beyond many of the current standard assumptions about economics, society, and the "good life" in making plans for the future. Success may have different meanings at different stages of life.

Whether one prefers to think of life as a problem and a struggle or an opportunity with great possible rewards, it is useful to remind ourselves that a human life has many different, though overlapping, components. In a typical lifetime human beings experience physical growth, learning, work, leisure, creative activity, family and community, hobbies and special interests, health and illness, and finally death. Yet even the most seemingly fundamental of these components—the typical life span in years of the individual—now appears subject to dramatic change, in either direction: much shorter through nuclear holocaust or environmental catastrophe, or much longer through breakthroughs in human biology.

As we have seen in the examples of the people interviewed in this book, one's life may be lived in a variety of contexts. Some people choose to inhabit big cities, others prefer a simpler life in a rural setting. One person may want to stay in one place, another to spend much of a lifetime traveling. One seeks privacy and relative isolation to concentrate on artistic or intellectual creation, another functions best in an active social milieu.

And, as individual lifetimes grow longer with a wider range of choices for many people, preferences will change over the life cycle. People may "retire" for a few years in their thirties or forties and find themselves productively engaged full-time in their seventies. Some teenagers leave the formal education treadmill to get a few years of work experience, and after that only spend hours in classrooms in short segments spread over a lifetime. Others may find age 50 a perfect time to invest four or five years in formal learning processes. And there will always be those who discover an inner call to some special kind of creative work at the most unexpected period in their lives.

It makes good sense for any person of any age to think hard about the overall sort of life he or she might prefer, about the aspects of that life which can be affected by conscious choice and personal action, and, finally, about what role work in return for income might appropriately play in such a life plan. Contrast that approach to planning to the standard point of view: "There is big demand now for lawyers and MBAs, so I will invest several years in getting that graduate degree." (If present trends continue, it won't be long before there are as many lawyers and accountants as there are secretaries now, with similar distribution of the rewards of money and prestige among these most common occupations. Meanwhile, Mrs. Patsy Edwards, out in California, has invented a lucrative new career field: counseling people on how to make good use of leisure time. Mrs. Edwards' earnings and satisfactions over the next ten years may turn out to be greater than those of the *average* 1982 graduate of a law school or business school.)

As a society we need to be paying much more attention to the processes by which intelligent, creative people find or create new opportunities, including new ways of earning a living. Creative people typically regard much of what they do as "play," and there is a message in that for all of us who have become conditioned to the idea that a person's work occupation is what gives life meaning. Let's look at some of the other things in life and the way they interact with our thinking and activity in the "work" realm.

Learning and Working and Learning

The very oldest readers of this book will remember how important it was considered in 1925 for a boy to have at least six or eight years of school under his belt before taking on his chosen line of work—unless his father was a farmer, in which case he'd already been working at his trade for a few years by the time his peers were getting out of school. It wasn't considered so important for girls, but even so a young woman had a little better status if she had gone beyond elementary school. A few boys went all the way through high school and became engineers or accountants or salesmen. The rare female high school graduate might go on to college to become a teacher or a nurse.

By 1945 you were not considered fit for the adult world of work until you had a high school diploma. By 1955 it was well understood that you would never get anywhere in life if you didn't have a college degree, and since 1975 all the best jobs have been going to people who had gone beyond college to graduate school. Ivar Berg has pointed out that by the 1970s about 80 percent of American college graduates held jobs that were previously done by people with considerably less formal education.

Until quite recently, this powerful social myth that a

certain number of years spent sitting in classrooms and reading books was somehow related to what you would be capable of doing later made sense to most people. That is, they believed it and accepted it—never mind that some of the most important contributors to society didn't fit the prevailing pattern. And so, our tax dollars built and staffed hundreds of new colleges and universities between 1960 and 1970; and even as late as 1978, many people still believed that if they put in the recommended time at the learning factories and acquired the right pieces of paper, they would get a good job.

The myth is now coming apart. Leaving aside changes in the economy and in technology, which sharply alter career opportunities, large numbers of people have become disenchanted with their expensive over-education. Indeed, more and more employers, according to recent surveys, are looking beyond academic credentials for something called "work experience." It hardly seems fair to someone who has devoted the first third of a lifetime acquiring the education those employers said they must have just a few years ago.

If you're under 21 and happen to have black or brown skin, your chances of getting a job, any job—*ever*—are about fifty-fifty. (We are talking about people whose level of formal education would have, in 1925, been considered appropriate for employment as an insurance salesman, plant foreman, or office worker.) If you happen to have a Ph.D. in English or history, your chances of getting any job that will allow you to make any appropriate use of all those expensive years of schooling are probably worse than the odds for the black teenager. According to a recent study* by Professor Ernest May of Harvard and Dorothy G. Blaney of the State Education Department of New York,

*Ernest May and Dorothy G. Blaney, *Careers for Humanists*, New York: Academic Press, 1981.

we are nearing the point where "a student enrolling in a Ph.D. program will have about as much chance of having a career as a professor as he or she would rolling a seven in a single cast of dice." The odds, according to this study, would be about five to one *against* ever obtaining a suitable job.

Of course, unlike the black teenager, the new Ph.D. will probably find some kind of job. Darcy O'Brien,* writing for *The New York Times Magazine* in a piece called "A Generation of 'Lost' Scholars," tells of one Ph.D. who was "supporting himself by doing odd jobs. He was a Fuller Brush man [a quite respectable occupation in 1935, by the way] and a telephone operator, and when I interviewed him, he was working for a government-sponsored group called Bet on a Vet, which helps veterans find jobs. His salary was $125 a week." O'Brien also interviewed William Miller, a Berkeley Ph.D., whose dissertation was "The Cultural Context of the Mythography of Milton's 'Comus.'" Miller now sells real estate. He told O'Brien, "By the time I got my doctorate, I could see how grim things were. I was pretty terrified for a while, but one day I sat down and decided what I wanted: money, free time, and to live in Berkeley. Next to literature, I love houses, so real estate was the obvious choice."

None of this fits with the myth, of course, but then neither did the impressive book-publishing career of William Targ. Targ was editor in chief of two very prestigious American publishing houses and worked over the years with such authors as Simone de Beauvoir, Samuel Beckett, Carl Sandburg, and Saul Bellow. Targ described the educational background that prepared him for his distinguished literary career:

"I've never really regretted being a high school dropout.

---

*Darcy O'Brien, "A Generation of 'Lost' Scholars," *The New York Times Magazine,* March 18, 1979.

The rigors and regimentation of school interfered with my indiscriminate reading; I was simply incapable of taking direction from teachers, unable to follow a circumscribed course of study or reading. No harm. I learned to lie glibly about my lack of education. Later, when anyone asked me where I was educated I would reply, 'Chicago.' Almost always, it was taken to mean the *University* of Chicago."

Targ continues: "The city of Chicago was my school: its writers and artists and newspapermen, the booksellers, the Art Institute . . . the Museum of Science and Industry, the Shedd Aquarium, the Adler Planetarium, the great parks, the Civic Opera, Grant Park, and the Gold Coast—the gothic beauty of the University of Chicago's buildings along the Midway. . . ."*

Learning does not take place only in schools.

Another example takes me back to my college days at Ohio Wesleyan University. One of my closest friends ran out of money in the middle of his sophomore year and took off for Chicago to look for work as a newspaper reporter. It was a sad day for those of us who loved John Callaway. It seemed that he and that modest midwestern college had a lot to give each other.

The next thing we heard, John was barely eking out a subsistence working the night shift on the police beat at Chicago's City News Bureau. Those of us sitting smugly in our cozy fraternity rooms laboring over Kierkegaard or Mendel and feeling sorry for our poor friend were just too naive to understand that the famous City News Bureau in Chicago was one of the most fertile fields of learning to be found, one that had nurtured major contributors to the American culture.

Since that time, John moved on to covering city hall and Mayor Daley for WBBM Radio, hosted for several years

---

Indecent Pleasures, New York: Macmillan, 1975.

the most popular and informative radio talk show in the Midwest, put together first-hand one of the most impressive documentaries in existence on the civil rights marches of the 1960s, briefly served as editor of a magazine, spent five years as a top executive of the CBS Radio Network in New York, went back to Chicago as a street reporter to get his feet wet in television, was shortly handed the job of creating the first news and public-affairs department at Chicago's public-television station, and now, among other things—always *among other things*—hosts one of television's most informative interview shows, gaining high marks from both the critics and his distinguished guests—people like Henry Kissinger, John Updike, and Jonas Salk.

John Callaway never went back to school. He never had the time. For the last 25 years he's been too busy reading thousands of pages every week, talking to anybody who will share knowledge or life experience with him, and *listening* carefully to what they have to tell him.

All this is not to say that it never makes sense to choose and follow through with a traditional institutional pattern of learning—if that is for sure the best route to doing what you want to do with your life. But the question needs to be raised, how often does the traditional, rigidly structured educational process move people not to the field or activity that will suit them best and provide the most personal satisfactions, but toward something *someone else* thinks will be best for them? It is a question worth considerable reflection as we observe more and more people making substantial investments of time and outrageous sums of money in educational processes which bear little or no relationship to the kinds of work they will be doing and the kinds of lives they will be living. Let me make it clear that I am not objecting to the countless benefits a person can gain from the usual processes of formal education. The problem arises when students are led to believe there is a relationship between that process and employment when so often there's not.

Not only is the old *system* for the transfer of useful information coming apart. More and more people are finding great benefit in taking smaller doses of formal learning at various intervals in the life cycle (for pleasure as well as for professional advancement) instead of accepting the idea that serious learning can occur only among people under 25 years of age. I am reminded of an old friend, Willis Heath, who, at age 45 after many years as a successful printer (a blue-collar field, for those who still care about such distinctions), decided to get a college education, didn't stop at that, and by age 50 had a Ph.D. in geography and a fascinating new career as a cartographer.

Fortunately, some traditional educational institutions, following the lead of the New School in New York and the U.C.L.A. extension college—two of the early pioneers in the field of adult education—are offering people instruction in things *they want or need to learn* at times and places suitable and convenient to widely varying life situations. Some others, like Simon's Rock College in Stockbridge, Massachusetts, recalling Robert Hutchins' mostly successful experiment in the 1940s, are accepting students for a basic four-year liberal arts education after only two years of high school. (One can now become a college dropout by age 16 if one so chooses, which is as it should be.) Even more flexible opportunities for learning are offered by groups such as the Learning Exchange, of Evanston, Illinois, and its many imitators all across North America. This sort of program provides the kind of "open market" in the field of learning that should have been a major component of any free society all along. Its working principle is simple and obvious: A structure is provided whereby people who have some expertise and the inclination to share it are brought together with people who want to learn this specialty—be it Russian language, yoga, or guitar construction. All or most of the exchange of learning takes place in people's living rooms or personal work spaces, with no expensive and inefficient investments in the bureaucratic trappings of faculty payrolls, questions of tenure, or large, expensive buildings housing huge collections of books, the vast majority of which are hardly read by anyone.

Learning is one of the most important and enjoyable experiences of living, but the idea of "an education" has become something else. We speak of getting an education as if it were a fixed package that can be bought. The market mentality quickly assigns greater value to a Harvard or Stanford label than to one from Oklahoma State. It's like a gown from Neiman-Marcus.

But, fortunately, only in the eyes of some people. Real life is much more complex, subtle, and surprising, as William Targ and John Callaway and countless others like them clearly demonstrate. As the old educational institutions cave in, more and more people seem to be making serious and constant learning an important ongoing dimension of their lives. And *enjoying* the process! Many of the people interviewed for this book have made it a point to find work that involves constant learning, rather than doing their learning in some separate, formal setting.

Stephan Eitzenhoefer, for example: "Most of my jobs have been a learning experience. I didn't know anything about computers, and now I'm working with computers and learning all about them. All that keeps on going. All my accounting experience came not from going to school . . . I went to college. I was a history major. But I worked business jobs. Somehow I was in the right place at the right time, and people hired me. I told them, 'Hire me. I can do

it. Just give it to me for a while, and I'll take care of it.'
That's how I got my experience. I'm always learning.
From every job I've ever done, I've learned something."

I asked Mike Galbraith how he learned cooking.

"From different chefs. You have to learn from chefs."
For Mike this has meant moving on when he learned what
he could from one chef. "You can't learn, especially in my
trade, if you stay with the same job. You'd just be stagnat-
ing."

Cobi Sucher learned a lot from her mother about fine
needlework. But the collection of well-thumbed books on
her shelf attests to a great deal of learning she has done on
her own. Terry Mollner taught himself about the commodities market. And Pat Lee learned to operate sophisticated word-processing systems in connection with one of
her temporary office jobs.

People who prefer a high degree of flexibility and autonomy in their work find ways to do their learning in a
similar fashion. It is worth emphasizing, for example, that
one of the best ways to acquire useful knowledge is
through reading. And reading requires free time. People
whose schedules do not include reasonable opportunities
for leisurely reading are missing out on an important, rewarding activity, and their success and satisfaction in many
dimensions of life may be directly affected by that lack.

There can be no doubt that learning and its close corre-
late, personal growth, are major factors in the degree of
satisfaction people find in their lives.

The quality of intimate relationships is another crucial
element of the "good life" for almost everyone. Just as we
have seen rapid changes in the sort of learning we need to
do and in the ways it can be accomplished, so have we
experienced dramatic changes in the ordinary intimate relationships among people in the past few decades. Divorce,
once considered something of a scandal, has become com-

monplace, giving rise to millions of single-parent families. At the same time we have seen an increase in the number of marriages in which both partners hold jobs. And it has become common for men and women to live together without marriage, in some cases for purely economic reasons with no romantic attachments. All of these changes have put new kinds of pressures on traditional forms of work organization, as have attitude changes in our culture—for example, the increased desire of many men to spend significant amounts of time with their children.

People whose livelihood depends on fitting into someone else's bureaucratic work routines have found it very difficult in many cases to manage these changed relationships, while others, like Barbara Keck, have made a clear decision that family comes first and work will be arranged to accommodate that top priority. One result of these changes is that more and more people are finding ways to do much or all of their work at home. Jerome Goldstein has solved the problem of integrating work and family life by employing several of his family members in his publishing business.

Increasing numbers of working mothers who are reluctant to place small children in day care are devising alternative ways to work that will allow them more time with their children. Sometimes the decision involves working less than full-time, or job sharing, or finding ways to live on a reduced income. Others, as we shall see, find that they can do what they do just as well at home as in an office.

The major push for flexible work arrangements—flextime, part-time jobs, job sharing—has come from women's organizations seeking especially to improve things for working mothers. Halcy Bohen, director of the Work Schedules Study of the Family Impact Seminar at George Washington University, stated the rationale rather succinctly: "For people with responsibilities in both job

and family, having some maneuverability in which to attend to needs in one context or the other—even a few
hours of flexibility at the beginning and end of each day—
may ease the logistical and emotional conflicts which can
arise between family and work."

While we have a long way to go, the efforts of groups
such as "New Ways to Work" in California, "Catalyst" in
New York, and the "National Council for Alternative
Work Patterns" in Washington, D.C., along with many ad
hoc women's groups all over the country have clearly
made significant gains. And we must pay more attention to
the fact that many *men* have as much interest in flexible
work options as women.

These changes taking place both in personal attitudes
and in traditional work organizations will slowly alter the
way we all view the organization of work, eventually making the variety of work arrangements described in this
book seem more acceptable. In the process more and more
children will have the advantage while they are growing
up of spending substantial time with both parents, unless
the two-parent family is finally overcome by the divorce
epidemic.

So much has been written in women's magazines, various commission reports, and scholarly articles about the
relationship between work and family life that I can add
nothing new. For readers seeking greater depth on this
issue, I highly recommend Rosabeth Moss Kanter's *Work
and Family in the United States,* a 1977 report from the Russell Sage Foundation, and *All Our Children.**

Before proceeding to other matters, it is worth pointing
out that intimate relationships other than within the family
also require free time, and are enhanced by flexible work
arrangements. A couple of people "getting to know each

---

*Kenneth Keniston and the Carnegie Council on Children, *All Our Children—
The American Family Under Pressure.* New York: Harcourt Brace Jovanavich, 1977.

other" can accomplish a lot more on a four-day weekend than compulsively trying to make the most of limited spare time from demanding, full-time jobs. Friendships as well, on all levels, are enriched by time for shared experiences instead of a quick lunch "to catch up."

We are accustomed to referring to all of the time not spent directly earning a living as leisure. But many people devote large blocks of time to work for which they get no pay. Sometimes it is household tasks that cannot be avoided, but sometimes it is creative work, with little or no financial reward, like Rowlie Sylvester's passion for restoring old boats for his Great Lakes Maritime Museum, or Terry Mollner's efforts to help organize worker-owned businesses. Or it may be community work—projects that may pay off in improvements in the quality of life for others but with no direct financial rewards for the person putting in the time.

It is interesting that many of our interview subjects make major commitments to non-income-producing projects that take a lot of time. Pat Lee has been active in political campaigns, Cobi Sucher spends time each year organizing and helping to manage the local farmer's market. These activities are not just hobbies. They provide a significant outlet for the expression of their personalities.

Then there are those time-consuming activities that have some less conventional economic payoff, like Mike Marien's gardening, which provides a substantial part of his food supply.

Quite a few of the people interviewed made it clear that time for being with friends was very important to them. The Levinsons and the Metzgers value time for travel. Felicia Kaplan gets carried away with exploring the city of Chicago, and Irma Wachtel needs time to practice her music and visit art museums.

As we explore the lives of these people who have chosen

to *design their own* lifestyles instead of having one imposed on them, two major themes emerge: integration and balance. The notion of a balanced life was expressed in one way or another in every interview, as was a desire to erase hard lines separating work, learning, family, play, and creative activity. Success for these people has little to do with the old idea of accumulating great wealth or social status and has a lot to do with a mode of living in which people feel internally integrated—"centered"—preferably spending most of their time in the company of others with similar values and aspirations.

10

Working at Home

Working at home is wonderful. Working at home means you don't have to get all gussied up to go sit in an office all day and look like you belong. It means you spend less money on clothes and transportation, makeup, and maybe a little more on the telephone service and equipment.

—Pat Lee

"If only there were more hours in a day!" How often have you heard this lament or made it yourself? Do you wonder how some people manage to get so much done in a day?

One answer may be that they don't waste time getting back and forth to their place of work every day, because they do their work at home. All those extra hours get used—for either work or pleasure. For some, of course, the two are the same thing.

During those times when I choose to define myself as a writer, I can be at work within 15 minutes of getting out of bed in the morning. Or I can wake up in the middle of the night with an idea and be at work in less than 5 minutes. Or because I don't have to appear someplace at some fixed time, I can spend the early morning hours in bed reading or watching Phil Donahue or enjoying my wife's good company, and ease into working when I'm ready for it.

At the other end of the day, there are people who work until midnight at the office to meet some important deadline and then drive for half an hour or wait for public transportation alone in the dark. A person who works at home can leave that neat, finally finished project on the desk and walk upstairs to bed.

John McClaughry is one of President Reagan's top advisers on domestic affairs, with a full-time job in the White House. John's previous affiliation was as director of the Institute for Liberty and Community. The Institute was located in Concord, Vermont, which is in that wild, sparsely populated third of the state Vermonters refer to as the Northern Kingdom. In fact, the Institute for Liberty and Community was essentially John McClaughry researching, writing, and consulting with people all over the country from a spare room of the log house he built with his own hands. Many of Ronald Reagan's radio scripts, in the years before he became president, were written in that house.

Most of us are familiar with the phrase "cottage industry." Our image is usually of some Scottish weavers in the Hebrides Islands who produce the famous Harris tweed cloth in their homes, or perhaps of a man who repairs clocks at home for a living. Those kinds of cottage industries continue to flourish. Jay Stryker told me he once had a machine shop operating in his apartment. There are many kinds of home-based industries; they have been the backbone of rural economies in much of the world for centuries.

But nowadays those of us in industrialized countries are living in what has been called an "information economy." Much of contemporary middle-class "cottage industry" in Europe and North America has to do with moving information around, as John McClaughry did. With the availability of small computers that can be plugged into immense data banks, word-processing equipment, and other devices, more and more people are setting up what Alvin Toffler calls the "electronic cottage."

The new cottage industries may be found in a handsome brownstone in Chicago's Lincoln Park, beside a swimming-pool in a rambling house in Palo Alto or Vancouver, or, like the Institute for Liberty and Community, in a remote rural area. One of my own great delights, when I moved from New York City to upstate farm country several years ago, was the discovery that the library in the nearby village (population 1,000) could get me any book in print within a few days through the interlibrary loan system. The headquarters of a cataloging operation for fabric designs that served clients all over the world was located in a much smaller village a few miles away.

I mention all this in part because of a common tendency of many people to think of going "back to the land" as a kind of regression to some primitive condition of life. The 1980 U.S. census figures show a steady migration of people out of the big cities and into rural areas, so some people are finding out that the country village ain't what it used to be. In case you haven't dropped into a country general store lately, you might be surprised to find *The Wall Street Journal* in the rack at the checkout counter— that is, if you get there early. By noon they'll all be gone.

A country setting often provides increased opportunities for that balance in life that so many people seek. Mike Marien prefers to work from 9 to 5. But since he does almost all of his work—reading, writing, and editing a monthly periodical—in the spare room of a cozy cottage in the country, he's got certain advantages that the office-bound person misses out on. If Mike gets stuck trying to think through something, he can always take a stroll in the woods, or swim in his pond, or do a little work in his garden until his unconscious mental processes have come up with the solution. Also it doesn't cost him $5 to $10 every time he goes to lunch.

Mike knows that he is most productive when he works alone, but his life is far from lonely. He frequently gives lectures and does consulting around the country, and he spends a few days each month in Washington, D.C. He attends several conferences and workshops of various kinds each year, and serves on a couple of boards. In short, he knows himself well enough to know that he sometimes needs the company of other people, and he schedules his time to provide it.

Cobi Sucher's day starts with an hour-long bicycle ride, even in cold weather. At the end of that ride she's at her place of work—which is also the place she just left—a former gas station that she has turned into a delightfully comfortable home and workshop. She says she needs to be outdoors getting vigorous exercise and taking in the sights of nature in order to get her creative energy flowing.

Not everyone prefers country living. The Marriotts' restaurant-consulting business involves clients throughout North America, and all of the work gets done in a lovely house overlooking San Francisco Bay.

A surprising number of business firms and other organizations whose address is given as a post-office box number are actually individuals or couples working at home.

Of course, "working at home" shouldn't always be taken literally. Some people do at least part of their work in unusual settings. On occasions "home" is Central Park for Pat Lee:

"You find your creativity isn't stuffed into a seven-hour context and a five-day work week. You're not stifled. You really expand. Your dimension is different. You're not identified by flat, square offices with flat, square furniture. You can work in the park. You can do very flat, square kinds of stuff like a word-processing recommendation or a more efficient time-utilization study in a traditional structure sitting in Central Park just as easily as you can do it sitting in an airless, windowless, cubby of an office. *And do it better.*"

Some of my own best ideas got written down at the beach, or while I was sitting over a leisurely cup of tea in a pleasant cafe. Flexibility of time and place is the major advantage to working at home.

Jane Marriott: "It's not taking the time to get dressed, getting in the car, driving to your office, answering your calls. There's a lot of time that we both would waste. We've had a lot of discussion about whether or not to get an office, even close by. We both like to be able to work at any hour, dressed in any way we want. It really works out for me. I just walk into the studio in a bathrobe, or I can do it in the evening. I have a lot of materials accessible."

Pat Lee: "It means if you want to work on a rainy day for 12 hours, and spend 12 hours in the sun the next day, you can. If you feel like sitting in your chenille bathrobe at midnight writing an employee handbook, and you really get into it and want to stay up till 4:00 in the morning doing it, that's terrific. You go ahead and do it. If you get really hot on a wage-and-salary study on a Saturday morning and you want to work through a whole weekend in order to take off Monday and Tuesday, you do it."

Jessica Lipnack: "The reason we bought this house was because of its size. We wanted to work at home. We use the two front-parlor rooms, and we each have individual studies on the third floor. I like having my work nearby. I find that very gratifying. We had an office for a long time, so I've also had the experience of going out of the house to work.

"We both really enjoy it in relation to our small children, because we've had a lot of access to the kids—they're seven months and three years. I'm nursing the baby, so it's made it possible for me to be one of the rare women who can work and nurse. That's a big issue for a lot of people with infants. So that's been wonderful. Being able to see them on and off all day and make choices about spending time with them has been great. You know, if something came up . . . if I wanted to spend some time, or if Jeff wanted to take Miranda off on a bicycle or something, we can do all of those things, and that is terrific."

Jay Levinson: "For me it's perfect, absolutely delightful. It's made our marriage better, not worse, because we're together more. This workroom doesn't look like a work-room, yet I have a lot of understanding from Pat and my daughter that work time is work time. I do that on Monday, Tuesday, and Wednesday. During these hours I need it at least fairly quiet. And for me it works."

Jay is in fact an expert on working at home, among other things, and presents workshops on it as one of his ways of earning money. He cautions that working at home is not for everybody. "I know people who have tried it and didn't like it." He also has found that the effect on a marriage may just as often be negative as positive—some people do better if they are not together all the time. "To some people, working at home is horrible. It's just the worst possible place to work. They find so many distractions and so much noise that they just can't get any work done. Some find they are lonely, that they miss the stimulation of being with other people, and they end up getting an office. Working at home in some cases is not all that good."

Scot Gardiner told me about a man who was trying to work at home, but found it too easy to be distracted. He used to linger endlessly daydreaming over morning coffee instead of getting down to work. He finally solved the problem by getting dressed each morning as if he were going to an office and walking out the front door precisely at 8:30. He went around to the back door, into his office, and down to work!

He told me of another friend who found it a terrible problem getting baby-sitters during the day. His wife worked outside the home, and the mothers of sitters didn't trust this man who "had nothing better to do than hang around the house all day." He finally had to get an office outside the house so they could keep a sitter.

Most people's problems are a bit less dramatic.

Michele Williams said, "I'm a soap-opera addict, so I get distracted by television. Since I have a studio apartment, my work area is part of my bedroom. A lot of times I just feel a need to get out of the house, but I have constant reminders of all the projects I need to develop."

Jessica Lipnack said, "The only thing that really bothers me are moments when I don't want the work to be sitting on the dining-room table."

The Applegath household gets even worse at times. As I write this, every room in our house is half-covered with papers, books, file cards. It looks terribly disordered, but in fact I can usually find what I'm looking for. Even so, there are times when something cannot be found in the mess, or other times when I can no longer stand my chaotic living environment. Then I declare a "mental health day" when I spend a couple of hours putting everything away, out of sight. This makes me feel that I have just moved into a new house, and my mind functions with much greater clarity. If your work is *always* in sight, it can get very depressing.

Mike Hassan was still getting used to working at home for the first time in his life when I talked with him:

"There are some real nice things to it, and there are some awful, awful dangers involved. It's real easy to dope off. Self-discipline is difficult. It's easy to go lie down and take a nap. It's nice, in that I know when it snows I'm not going to have to worry about whether I can get my car out or not. In another sense, though, I miss going into the office.

"I found myself for a time needing some kind of structure. For years I made a daily trip to the post office. Every morning I'd go to the post office and then have a cup of coffee someplace. Then I'd come back and do some work. I guess I just need to add a little bit of structure to my time.

"Another thing about working home when there's a small child around is that when 2:30 rolls around, you can pretty much hang up whatever it is you're doing. That complicates it somewhat."

Sometimes working at home can make life very complicated. The August 1980 issue of *In Business* magazine carries an article by author's agent and writer Elyse Sommer entitled "The Pleasures and Pitfalls of a Business at Home," which includes this description:

> One family with a growing investment business rented a three-story brownstone. The top floor is strictly family, the basement houses the office and staff of five—the middle floor is sort of a hybrid with dining and living rooms doubling for business conferences. Since the family includes four youngsters under ten, and domestic as well as business help, things get kind of hectic for these young business tycoons. So they have an away-from-office-home getaway as their own romantic hideaway for lunches and occasional evenings.

People who choose "working free" tend to be very creative. And often that includes convincing some company that their work can be done just as well in *your* home as in *their* office or factory. Steve Schulze recently left Boston for the free-lance life in the country. He's an expert at one of the most important engineering tasks in the booming electronics business: designing printed circuits. He now does the work on contract in his home. Schulze said the electronics business is in "a really healthy state," and added, "I'm sure that there is plenty of work out there for free-lancers."

We'll learn more about some interesting developments along these lines in our chapter on employers. Some of the smarter ones are discovering benefits for themselves in arrangements for people to work at home.

We've mentioned a pretty wide range of kinds of work that are compatible with the home workplace: writing, research, videotape services, all sorts of consulting, counseling, teaching, electronics engineering—the possibilities are endless. Jay Levinson lists many more in his delightful books, *Earning Money Without a Job* and *555 Ways to Earn Extra Money,* and women's magazines and daily newspapers regularly suggest new home-based businesses. It's definitely a strong trend, and growing stronger. Elyse Sommer concludes, "Those who find the at-home lifestyle compatible with their business, temperament, and lifestyle will find the will and the way to make it work."

11

Security—The Future

I think once you get the knack of knowing that you're not going to be starving to death . . . how could you in this country? They wouldn't let you if you tried, right? Isn't that right?

—Cobi Sucher

One of the fundamental parts of the traditional work ethic is the idea that if an employee serves his or her employer faithfully for many years, his future will be "insured." That means the employee can look forward to a time of retirement with sufficient income to live in reasonable comfort. Current financial realities have made many retirement plans entered into years ago when the value of the dollar was much greater inadequate, but regardless, most regularly employed people will have some steady income when they retire.

By contrast, very few of the people interviewed for this book have made any formal arrangement for setting aside funds for old age. Various financial planners and government agencies recommend that self-employed people set up some form of systematic saving for the future, and indeed a few of our people have such plans in effect. But most do not.

Here we find one of the fundamental differences between people who choose to be "working free" and the rest of us. The difference can be pretty well summarized by saying that these people *live very much in the present.* "I just take one day at a time" was a theme I heard frequently in the interviews. Francine Rizzo said, "I'm not afraid. And that's what makes me different. I have the same everyday cares as other people do, but overall I'm not afraid of what is going to happen. I'm not looking into the future—I'm living in the moment."

We have already discovered that these people have a different view of risk than most other people. Perhaps the ultimate risk they take is having enough confidence in themselves to assume that they will still be able to earn whatever money they need when they are old. Indeed, John Peitz, in his seventies, lives quite comfortably with a combination of small Social Security benefits and the income from his bread baking and some occasional typesetting jobs he does at home.

Most of the people whose stories are told in this book don't give much thought to the time when they will no longer be working. It would probably be better if they paid more attention to the fact that any of us may face health problems in the unknown future, and that means that some self-employed people may become hopelessly dependent in the event of severe physical disability. Nonetheless, this book is not meant to be prescriptive or judgmental about other people's choices, but rather to learn what some of the coping strategies are outside the "system." And so, we will listen to a few of them talk about their thoughts on security and the future.

Stephan Eitzenhoefer, at age 31, had no trouble explaining what security means to him:

"There is no security. People have got to look at that, too. Well, maybe there is, but it's just got to be personal.

It's got to be what you are deciding for yourself. Anything can change at any time, any day, any minute. And if *you* are secure, you can go with it. If you're not scared. If you're ready for anything that's going to come across, you can just keep going."

I asked, what about the future?

"I don't know. I think in long-range terms at times, but it's so ambiguous to me that I don't know. I've learned how to survive just by going and doing things. I just keep doing that. And whatever is going to happen in the future is probably going to be pretty much the same general concept or style. As I told you, I don't mind what comes next."

What Steve had told me earlier was: "There's always something I'll be able to do. There is always something I *will* do. Nothing ever doesn't appeal to me—especially if I want to *eat!*"

Mike Galbraith: "Well, I feel secure in what I'm doing right now." Jane: "Clothes on your back, a place to live." Mike: "And medical coverage. Other than that we're pretty secure in what we're doing. Cooks' jobs are a dime a dozen. I'll never be down. I'll never be out of a job. People are eating out more and more these days. As long as people like to eat there will be cooking jobs."

Mike and Jane, in their twenties, are saving some money to be invested. Mike: "I don't know whether it's to buy a house, or invest in a small restaurant with someone else— to try to start out and get bigger and bigger. I'd like to try something like that, but it takes a lot of money." Jane: "If we didn't move around so much, we'd have a little more saved up."

As for the longer-term future, Jane offered: "I think eventually we're going to have a restaurant somewhere, with a nice small home with a couple of kids. Mike will be the chef." Mike: "That's very long-term." Jane: "That's the long-term future for me. That's what I'd like to see myself doing eventually." Mike: "You have to be mentally ready for all that, and *financially* ready."

Steve Eitzenhoefer is young and single. Mike and Jane Galbraith are even younger, married, but with no children to support as yet. Jay and Patsy Levinson and Bob and Jane Marriott, on the other hand, are in their forties. The Levinsons are raising children, as are Jeffrey Stamps and Jessica Lipnak. Surely, concerns about security and the future weigh differently on these older, more experienced people, especially with the responsibilities that come with children. Surely? Well, maybe.

Jay Levinson: "I'd like to maintain this lifestyle [working only three days a week] indefinitely. But I'm sure that I'll change my opinion, because when I was 22 years old, I set an ambition for myself that got changed by the time I was into my early thirties. But for now, three days a week is fine. It's a lot of fun."

When Jay talks about the future, he plans to be even more footloose and unstructured, not less. He is certainly not making plans to retire to Sun City to play shuffleboard:

"I'm hoping . . . here's an ambition I have that I share with Patsy. . . . We always want to have a place in Marin County, but we would like to live in Europe again for a year. We'd like to trade a house, in Hawaii for a year, in Israel, Australia, places like that. We've traded houses in the past, and it really works. It makes for a wonderful vacation all the way around.

"Patsy's a few years away from writing about what she does. She can write a textbook on it. She has written for medical journals and she can start doing that again in a few years. She's paying some dues right now. And I'm aligning my life to be more literary and less advertising so that I can do the same things. I'd like to get to the point where I'm totally independent from having to be in any one place, so we can live away from Marin a year at a time without giving up residence here."

Bob and Jane Marriott:

Jane: "Neither one of us has ever been very savings-oriented. Worrying about security has never been a preoccupation for either of us."

Bob: "We'd like to maintain our way of life, being able to do the kinds of things we want to do and like to do, and live in a place we like to live in—and at the same time to be building something for the future. But we're not really—at least I'm not—oriented that way as much as I should be, or as much as Janie thinks we should be. And I know she's right. I agree in theory that we can't do this forever, but at the same time I want to be able to enjoy life as we're living it rather than thinking too much of how we're going to survive the declining years."

Jane: "I've changed in the last five years, and I think my motivation now is probably—even though I don't like to admit it—I think I've come to a place where I want to have some kind of balance and security. I'm usually a very up person, very energetic, but I don't think I've had a good balance. I'm really happy now. I'd like to be able to sustain it . . . and I'm worried. Sometimes I wonder, 'Gee, are we always going to be able to live this way?' "

It is interesting that the traditional male-female difference on the matter of security versus adventure persists, even among people with quite unorthodox lifestyles. But, as always, there are major individual differences.

Jessica Lipnak (nursing one infant, with a two-year-old underfoot): "When I think about security, the first thing that comes to mind is *emotional* security. I don't know. I'm not terribly hung up on it. I grew up in a family that had very little money, and somehow everything worked out, even when there were tons of problems. I don't know . . .

we don't have savings accounts or anything like that. We do have health insurance—we have children."

Past experience, whether it involves a sense of security imparted by parents or perhaps insecurity in early years, seems to color present attitudes. Sebastian Moffatt spoke about such things:

"Especially, of course, now that I have a family . . . you can't help but think more about security and the future. I once spent a year traveling in Europe. I lived for over a year on $600. That's poverty . . . I've experienced it. I'm not afraid of it.

"Another thing is my parents. They are not wealthy, but they're comfortably middle class. That's really important to understand, because, really, it's like my life insurance, you know. Having middle-class parents isn't 'money in the bank,' but I could always call on them—even though I don't. For reasons I don't understand, I've never asked them for money, and they didn't put me through school or anything else. But I know I always have that to fall back on. When I've participated in small group sessions, there's a big dividing line between the individuals who have parents who can always put them up with a place to sleep or help out if things really got bad, and people who simply have nothing to fall back on. It's a huge difference between individuals."

Moffatt's vision of his future is very tangible:

"I would like to have some *land*. Land to me would be everything. The land would give me a place to leave my things when I want to travel; to develop a community; to subsistence farm, if I really couldn't get work; and to sell if I needed instant capital for any major emergency. So it's better—especially given the state of the economy—it's better than any insurance I could possibly buy. A little bit of land is what everybody wants, understandably."

Well, not *everybody*. I asked New Yorker Pat Lee, "Do
you ever think about when you're old, and how you're
going to pay for your food and rent when you're 70?"

"No. I think about it. Don't get me wrong. But I'm
healthy now, and I hope that I'll be healthy then. I'm
vested with U.S. Plywood. That's $100 a month I'll get
when I'm 65—which will be worth a good $10 by that time.
I don't give it a lot of thought. I don't expect to be a
burden on society. But I don't worry about it. Who knows
if I'm going to be around then?

"Maybe, though, I'll be a very famous artist by then, and
all my little charcoal drawings will be going for $100,000
and I may not need to worry about it. There are so many
variables. I'm so receptive to change—I wasn't always; I
used to be really threatened by it. I find that the more
receptive I am and the more flexible I am, the more opportunities there are to make money and to support myself."

Francine Rizzo is pretty "flexible" too:

"I went over to somebody the other day who is very
concerned about the future and I put my arms very lov-
ingly and compassionately around him and said, 'Don't
worry about the future. There isn't any.' You know, there
are cultures of the world that don't have a word or a tense
that represents the future . . . the Chinese don't have a
future tense in their language, and they've been going
strong for thousands of years.

"I'll tell you how the future hit me. When I was maybe
21 years old, I was working in a company in New York.
They just got a new group plan for something or other—
pension—and they handed me this very beautiful paper
with a seal. It said, 'You will receive $38.12 every month
starting in the year 2004.' I said, 'I quit.' You know what I
mean? And that's what turned me off to the future—Social
Security and all that. If I was worried about my old age, I'd

be working in a company and building up my pension, but I don't think I'm going to be here. I'm not going to be a hundred years old; and as long as I keep just a little bit lean, I'll have my faculties to the end, even if I do live to be 100."

Some people think that not making concrete plans and arrangements for one's later years is irresponsible. But these do not sound like irresponsible people. Not one of them suggests that they expect someone else to take care of them when they are older. And we've learned enough about these people by now to be pretty sure that none of them would be comfortable for long in a relationship of major dependency.

This discussion inevitably brings us back to the matter of risk taking. And Jessica Lipnak had something especially interesting to say that reveals a very special way of viewing the future:

"The whole world seems to me to be in such precarious balance that it's all a risk. The real risk comes from not doing something to help change that.

"I don't feel that we're taking risks. I think the real risk is to just concentrate on making money. I think that people who are not really banking on the future are the ones who would appear to be the most conservative. I think that we really need to change things quite significantly. We can't go on this way. And unless people are working toward solutions, then they're the ones who are taking a risk."

We opened this chapter with a quote from Cobi Sucher, so we'll let her have the last word:

"There's enough feeling of security, I guess, about what I'm doing. It seems that every time I run out of work somebody will show up at the door and give me another job—even a five-dollar job. So I've survived, I really have.

"My daughter is in a panic sometimes about whether she

is going to survive. And she's so busy, busy, busy, having jobs and making money. I said 'Jackie, just look back in your own life, and you can see that you've *always* survived, you've *always* had a job. You've never starved. What are you so worried about? You're going to be taken care of.' But that's a spiritual thing. It has nothing to do with economics really. It's a spiritual attitude. You know you're going to be taken care of."

12

Getting Your Act Together

The journey of a thousand miles begins with a single step.
—Lao-tzu

We were sitting on the upper deck of Rowlie Sylvester's "Nikanong" marina in the harbor of South Haven. It was a sunny August morning, and we watched the constant traffic of pleasure boats in and out of the harbor below as we talked. The conversation turned to how one goes about making the change from a standard job to "working free." I asked Rowlie if he had any advice for people who might be thinking of making that move.

"Nope. No advice. But I do have a story about an old friend. . . ."

Rowlie has quite a few stories and some fairly unusual friends, so I was pretty sure what was coming would be something special:

"I got acquainted with Studs Terkel down in Selma, Alabama—marching along with Martin Luther King in those days, and singing 'We shall overcome.' Sometime later, Studs came to visit me in South Bend. He said, 'I'm going to try something different. I've been in this broadcasting business all my life, and now I'm going to try being a writer. I'm going to try my interview technique and see what it would look like written out.'

135

"He was getting some encouragement from a good publisher's editor, so, instead of going to college to take
courses on writing, he just started doing it. He went to a
writers' workshop for three weeks, and then he was a
writer! He wrote one best-seller right after another, and
you can't stop him now. Of course, he has a special talent
with people and a tape recorder. He has a very nice way of
drawing them out, of somehow getting them to speak what
is deepest within themselves."

It's rarely that easy, and there's only one Studs Terkel.
But it's a real nice story. And it illustrates an important
point. Many people assume that if they're going to do
something different from what they're doing now as a way
of earning a living, the first thing they have to do is to save
up a lot of money so they can go back to school for two or
three years. Sometimes that's appropriate, but more often
people do what Studs did. They take a close look at their
talents and experience and figure out a way to do something different with those tools—or maybe do just about
what they've been doing, but without a boss over them.

In any case, you don't always need a certificate from
some formal institution that says you are "qualified" to do
something. If you're going to practice medicine or law,
O.K. But you want to go from writing corporate annual
reports to writing a book? Why not just do it? Want to start
counseling people on how to manage their lives or their
money? There are lots of career consultants and investment consultants out there earning a living because they
learned what they needed to know in their own best way.
Terry Mollner taught himself everything he needed to
know about the commodities market. I have never taken
any courses on writing past high school journalism. Dorri
Jacobs has a Ed.D. in dance and earns most of her income
now doing career and life-plan counseling and writing.

Then we have Bob Marriott, who did advertising work

for an agency and now does it for himself; Pat Lee, who learned all about office management systems from years of working on company payrolls and now shares her knowledge and skills as a consultant; or Irma Wachtel, who did computer programming from 9 to 5 for years but now does it only when she feels like it, or needs the money.

If I'm making it all sound easy, it isn't. My point is that you may not have to put yourself through a whole lot of extra formal education to make the sorts of changes we've described. Of course, if the idea of being a student for a while has its own appeal for you, and you have the money, by all means do it.

I chose to begin this chapter with the question of "credentials" because that story about Studs Terkel was such a nice one—but also because this issue seems to be a major hang-up for many people. And what it mostly boils down to is that we've all been brought up in a bureaucratic society that worships formal institutions and structures, and we don't know how to evaluate our own *experience*. Anyone who has earned a living for a few years knows how to do *something* that is useful to other people. So we must begin by looking at all of our accumulated knowledge and experience, skills, and talents, and thinking about what they add up to *outside the context of one's present organization*. It's just like writing a really good résumé, only when you get it all together, you're going to be the person hiring this talented individual. You're going to hire yourself, and then you're going to go out and sell your talents to somebody *on your terms* this time.

A few readers of this book may be just out of school, but I think it is safe to assume that most of us have lived a few years in the conventional work environments. All of us have acquired some valuable skills. And it is important to remember that many of your most valuable and tradeable skills may have been acquired outside your place of work.

If you did some volunteer work that helped to raise money for the restoration of an old building in your town, you have learned something about sales work and fund raising. If you nurtured two helpless infants toward becoming competent adults, you have demonstrated priceless skills that can be transferred to other fields if you want to use them in another context: A part-time job in a day-care center? Counseling confused teenagers? Planning parties for other people's kids? Organizing a resale shop for children's clothing? You may even have learned valuable skills on your present job. Schoolteachers are sometimes amazed to discover how much *management* talent they have acquired running a daily classroom—to say nothing of the impressive self-discipline required to read and grade students' homework.

The point of all this, of course, is that all of us have already done some important preparation for our next move, but perhaps without being really aware of it. It may help to write down a list of *all* skills you have. (Do you talk comfortably and effectively in small groups—in front of bigger audiences? Are you extremely good at organizing details? Do you write wonderful letters? Are you the one who always *organizes* the annual vacation? Do you just happen to have a wonderful relationship with the keyboard of a computer console, a gourmet cookbook, or a video camera?) Whatever your particular combination of experience, skills, and special knowledge, chances are good that you can put together some combination of those things— maybe adding some new skill you want to acquire—in a way that will enable you to earn a living. Maybe it will be two different part-time jobs, or maybe your set of skills combined with different ones of a good friend could be the basis for a consulting business, a writing and editing service, a child-care program, or any of a thousand other possibilities. People all around you are creating new careers for themselves every day.

Having a good inventory of your work-related skills and experience is only one part of a much more encompassing task that must be dealt with thoroughly at the outset or it will cause serious problems later on. The philosopher's version of that task is "Know thyself." That, of course, is something we may spend a lifetime working at. For our purposes, let's just say, "know yourself as thoroughly as you can." Check out the illusions, the unrealistic fantasies. Run them down. Where are they coming from? What are your usual energy patterns? How much self-discipline do you have? What is your *real* reason for wanting to leave your present job?

This last item may be crucial. In a fascinating book called simply *Authority,** Richard Sennett describes one of the common self-delusions that keeps people locked into complex rejection-dependency relationships with the authority figures in their lives. These are people who have some sort of need to keep a pattern of rebellion going against authority figures. Remove the authority figure and they are lost, the "meaning" in their life is gone.

It is not easy to shift attitudes, habits, and lifestyle from a situation in which you follow someone else's directions, show up at a place of work at regular times to put in full days, and put out energy toward meeting someone else's goals, to a situation in which you make all the decisions, from the big ones to the small ones, like what time to get out of bed in the morning.

It is not *easy*, to repeat the old cliché, but it is *simple*. Outlining some clear steps can help in making the transition, but the ease or difficulty with which any individual

*Richard Sennett, *Authority,* New York: Knopf, 1980.

does it depends almost entirely on personal values, habits, attitudes, fears and insecurities, level of energy, degree of motivation, and more. In short, most of the obstacles to gaining greater freedom in one's working life do not lie in the "system." They lie within the individual. I cannot provide the perfect solution to *your* situation. I can only suggest some guidelines and tools. You get to do all the work.

That work, and it is very demanding, must begin with a completely thorough and realistic self-assessment. Just who are you, what do you want out of life, and why aren't you getting it now? Some readers may have already done a lot of work on this set of questions and have a clear notion of their personal values, goals, and priorities, as well as their personal strengths and weaknesses. Those who know themselves well and feel ready to start making the necessary moves may wish to skip the next few pages, but what follows is fundamental to success in "working free." More and more people are embarking on paths of self-discovery and autonomous action, even though, as we have said, it is difficult work. Those of us who find ourselves having to work day after day in the company of people *whose neuroses run them* have a special sense of how important the work is.

What are the best tools for self-understanding? What is "best" will, of course, vary with each individual. Mike Pavilon did research for his MBA thesis which showed that people who had been through some intensive psychotherapy progam are more productive and creative in their work. Mike gained a lot of insight about himself through "Outward Bound" programs. Some people have discovered the most important facts about themselves through meditation (although a much larger number seem to have substituted some guru or other for the previous authority figure in their lives and in the process have been sold some passivity program to make them even more receptive to the guru's manipulations). Some people are able to respond constructively to the brutal confrontations of "est" or gestalt therapy. Others gain insights through long conversations with trusted friends who are not afraid to respond honestly to difficult questions.

So many books on the subject are available that at least one is bound to stimulate some new insight in your personal quest. They range from philosophical treatises like Alan Watts's *The Wisdom of Insecurity* or Rollo May's *The Courage to Create,* to very practical books of systems and exercises like John Crystal's *Where Do I Go From Here with My Life?* or Richard Bolles's *What Color is Your Parachute?*

All kinds of workshops are available at various times of the year all over North America on subjects ranging from "values clarification" to "making choices," to "life and career planning," to my own workshops, "Finding Meaningful Work," "Working on Your Own Terms," and "Inventing Your Own Job." I have listed a few contact sources for these programs in Research and Resource Information at the end of the book.

Knowing yourself means many different things. It means knowing what is most important in your life. It means ordering priorities, knowing your particular strengths and weaknesses, knowing what you can safely compromise, and for how long, in the interest of gaining something else you need—and knowing which compromises of your values and priorities will be deadly. It means knowing something about other people, too. What kinds of people stimulate your creativity and productivity? Who brings you down? For some people, knowing oneself includes having some kind of a plan for the future. For others, the future will take care of itself if we only keep our attention well focused on what we are doing *now.*

One thing is certain. No individual's "Know thyself" process is going to come out exactly like somebody else's. Let us remind ourselves once again: We are all different.

And those differences can enhance that part of our lives devoted to earning a living if we choose to make it come out that way. Unfortunately, many people choose to accommodate others *too much,* to compromise their own best qualities *too much,* because somebody else causes them to believe that they have to in order to survive. In some cases this may be true. Wage slaves and soldiers have very limited options.

By now it should be clear that you will waste less time and energy, and be more successful at what you finally choose to do, the more you know about yourself. A rerun through the preceding pages with special attention to the degree of self-understanding exhibited by the people interviewed will confirm this crucial fact.

Since the point of all this self-exploration has to do with finding a new way to put bread on your table and pay the rent, the next crucial step is to clarify your relationship with *money.*

You really have to know how important money is in your life, and how much you will need, first, just to survive and take care of the other people dependent on you, and second, to live the way you want to. And while you're at it, get some clear idea of how long you are willing to stay at the survival level in order to get what you want ultimately. Some people are not too uncomfortable alternating the two modes from time to time. You'd better know ahead of time whether you're one of them, or if you always have to have five or ten grand in the bank in order to sleep at night (and therefore be creative and productive during the time you're supposed to be awake). The big question here is what sort of trade-off you *choose* to make between money and free time. If you understand the dimensions of that one, and if you understood that it is your choice, money will not be one of your problems most of the time. Money is a problem for *everyone* sometimes. Remember when

Bunker Hunt couldn't pay for all that silver he thought he owned?

Carefully tracking your money requirements can be a very revealing exercise. Just holding a regular job costs money you wouldn't otherwise spend. How much of your current income, for example, goes for certain kinds of clothes, or the cleaning of them, required for looking "respectable" or "with it" in somebody else's eyes? How much do you spend on gas and car maintenance or public transportation getting back and forth to work? How much do you end up spending on entertainment because your work is such a drag that you have to take yourself into some fantasy world a couple of times a week? It's interesting that people who make the transition to working on their own terms consistently say that they are spending a lot less money on entertainment because they are enjoying themselves more *all the time.*

How much money do you spend each month doing things that "are expected" of a person in your job category? Many people actually live in expensive neighborhoods they don't particularly like, or because of the "convenience" of getting to the office in a reasonable amount of time.

When you really analyze the money issue, you may very well be surprised by how much it's costing you in hard dollars to live somebody else's kind of life. You may find out that you don't need nearly so much money as you now think you do once you aren't obliged to spend just to satisfy other people's needs. That same money can be the gravy for all the things you didn't think you could afford.

Quite a few people "working free" do a lot of bartering for the things they need. A self-employed psychotherapist I know trades an hour of therapy time for an hour of household maintenance work on a regular basis with one client. Artists will often trade a painting for legal services or dental work. You might be able to write speeches for some corporate executive in return for using his company's WATS line and copying machine. The possibilities are endless. In fact, bartering has become so widespread that the IRS is now trying to get a handle on it.

If you're going to get serious about making the switch from 9 to 5 to "working free," be sure you have a clear idea about how you will handle the money issue. Two books—Slater's *Wealth Addiction* and Phillips's *The Seven Laws of Money*—will help to clarify your picture.

Before we leave the subject of money, let's go back to "security." No matter what you think your attitude is, you'll feel better if you can salt away some money in some form for your old age or for a run of bad luck. You'll sleep better at night, and your family and friends will like you better when the hard times come. A few suggestions. You will be spending a certain part of your income every month for the rest of your life on a place to call home. Whatever that monthly figure is for you, if it goes out as rent, in 20 years you own nothing. Can you find a way to save up a down payment so those inevitable monthly checks will be paying off a mortgage?

Can you barter something for the services of a good investment counselor who can tell you whether your occasional surplus income should be put into the stock market, a mutual fund, bonds, or Treasury bills? Your local banker can tell you everything you need to know about the various kinds of retirement plans for self-employed people and others not covered by company retirement programs. One neat trick, if you have more than one regular source of income, is to put all the income from *one* of those sources aside as savings.

It is impossible to overestimate the value of a good tax accountant who understands the special needs of people who work in unconventional ways. When you move from working for someone else to doing it your way, you may very well be able to deduct all kinds of expenses you might not think of yourself. And if you're ever audited, you've got someone else to explain to the IRS the tangled financial affairs of the free-lancer, or person with five part-time jobs, or whatever.

Once you are satisfied that you know yourself pretty well and have figured out how much money you really need, it's time to figure out such things as where you want to live and under what conditions, how much of your time you want to devote to earning a living, and what you want to do with the rest of your time. Then devise a specific plan that allows some flexibility, because once you start doing things on your own terms instead of someone else's, you may discover unexpected opportunities in your path, new directions you want to pursue. But clearly some discipline about specific priorities and steps to be taken will be required, for as Richard Sennett has pointed out, "To look for freedom through autonomy creates a terrible anxiety." In short, the goal has got to be something a whole lot more specific than just "freedom."

In my own case, I decided some years ago that I placed a high value on flexibility and variety in my life—being able to go to different places, do different kinds of things. The solution for me was to become a writer, because free-lance writing can be done almost anywhere under the most varied circumstances. I was particularly delighted the first summer I discovered I could actually get some good work done sitting on the dock at a beautiful Canadian lake, while my daughter Molly frolicked in the water nearby.

There was another very important element in my plan. I decided I never again wanted to be totally dependent on only one sort of work to earn income. My plan was to begin immediately developing at least three, and preferably four or five, different ways to earn money. It took some time. And there were uncomfortable periods when *none* of my projects were paying the bills, or, while trying to do too many things at once, my life took on a rather frantic quality. But the demands of this approach and several difficult years forced me to develop some self-discipline and ordering of priorities that now serves me well.

The great advantage of this strategy is that I am never locked in to one "career." If one thing isn't working out well, or if I'm getting bored, I can choose to drop it and put more time into one of my other projects, without feeling that I'm making a major "career change." The possibilities are wide and the specifics will naturally vary from person to person, but *the idea of having more than one way to earn money is fundamental.* It is a strategy I particularly recommend to young people who are just beginning to think about the world of work and how they will earn their living. Things have a way of changing very fast and the person with only one sort of skill may end up in a dead-end situation at a very inconvenient time in life.

You may find it easier to spend most of your time doing what you really want to do if you are not under the intense pressure of always having to earn all your income from that one source. As we know, the arts are kept going by people who, for the most part, earn a living from part-time jobs as typists, waiters, and cab drivers. And a person who may want to do some creative work in the computer field may earn some money doing routine programming on a free-lance basis. One man I know accumulates the money he needs by doing small jobs at modest pay for about a dozen nonprofit organizations. Pat Lee has done everything from catering to housecleaning when she becomes bored with office work. It's interesting that people often find these so-called menial jobs rather fun when they are doing them for someone else and getting paid for it, and when they know they don't have to do it *all the time.*

Once you have your plan in mind, it would be wise to break it down into easily manageable steps, so that you can periodically check yourself out on what parts of the plan are working and what parts need some adjustment. That permits you to make a major rearrangement if you need to before you get too deeply committed.

Finally, your plan will certainly work out more gracefully if you don't rule out the possibility of going back to a more standard work structure sometime in the future if it should become important to do so. Such a reversal need not be a defeat but could provide some breathing space for planning another, later departure. I like Rowlie Sylvester's way of thinking about this issue:

"You realize that things go in cycles, and there may be a period when it fits your mood not to be in the structure of the shop or the office or whatever—that you want to do something individually. However, that doesn't have to last forever. It's one of your options to try an individualistic way. Then later on you may want to get that umbrella over your head for a while, get some income coming in. That may suit your purposes even more. This doesn't mean that you've got to go for the pension and for the lifetime gig with an employer and retire at 65 with a gold watch. That's just a cliché. And you don't have to live strictly by the terms of a cliché—either in freedom or in a structure, and they are just clichés. Both of them have a lot of possible variations.

"But nothing has to be forever. That's the main thing. It's just as bad to say 'I can never go back to work,' or 'I can never take a 9 to 5 job and be on a payroll'—that's a definition of yourself that's probably going to drive you crazy—on the other hand, if you have that security for a while, it's just as ridiculous to say, 'Well, I could never take the chance of going out and trying something on my own.'"

Here are a few more basic principles to bear in mind that will make your transition to "working free" more graceful and successful:

Information: The world is full of information that can be directly useful in executing your plan. Smart people take a lot of time to do thorough homework before committing themselves to action. You probably know what many of your major sources of information will be, and I've listed my choices of some of the best ones at the end of this book. But the best sources are other people who have done something like what you have in mind. Seek them out and ask a lot of questions. They'll enjoy the process and will probably give you a lot of good information and encouragement. People love to talk about what they've been successful at doing. And don't be shy about probing the problems they've encountered and how they solve them. It may save you some unpleasant surprises, and you can gain confidence from someone else's experience.

Equipment: Get properly set up *from the beginning.* If you don't have the money to buy the word-processor or some other tool you really need to do the job right, seriously consider getting a loan to pay for it. Having all the right tools at your fingertips from the start will greatly increase your self-confidence, efficiency, and enjoyment. Be sure you have a comfortable, convenient, efficiency-inspiring work space, with everything you may need close at hand: proper lighting, file cabinets, bookshelves. A lot of good intentions and fine talents have gone down the drain for lack of a proper work environment.

Self-discipline: Get in the habit of knowing what you want or need to do, and do those things *first.* Establish regular work habits that suit you best. Get rid of destructive attitudes and habits, and replace them with constructive ones. Some time and money invested with a professional counselor might pay off in improved productivity, more enjoyable work time, and more free time. At the very least, study and apply the excellent advice in Alan Lakein's book *How to Get Control of Your Time and Your Life.*

Learning: Get in the habit of experiencing all of life as a learning process and keeping track of what you learn. Carry a notebook with you at all times, and file those notes where you can easily retrieve them when you want them. (Scot Gardiner takes notes on computer cards during conversations, codes each one, and files each in his computer under "key words.") On trips, take along a tape recorder to capture those special creative ideas that come when you have the leisure for relaxed reflection. Learn from everyone and everything you can. You cannot know in advance when that information may turn out to be useful.

Flexibility: Change is the essential nature of reality. Your attitude can make change either a burden or an opportunity. A narrow life plan leads to more anxiety and frustration than a wide-ranging, flexible one.

Social interaction: Learn what situations and people tend to stimulate and enhance your *creativity* and *productivity,* and spend your time in those contexts rather than burying yourself in the familiar and comfortable routines of your past. People who work alone a lot should view social occasions, at least in part, as investments in their own mental health. That includes spending the least time possible with people who *bring you down.*

Be yourself: Every person is different. The biggest obstacle you will confront in the effort to manage your own life will be the opinions, attitudes, values, and advice of other people in your environment. It is essential not only to know yourself, but to *be yourself every day.* It will be helpful to spend most of your time in the company of people who appreciate your values, priorities, and interests. *Never underestimate what you are capable of doing.* And don't unrealistically *overestimate.* We all have limits.

Resources: Learn to identify and use all of your personal resources and any outside resources available to you. A friend's special knowledge or contacts can improve your efficiency. Someone you know may have a piece of equipment that would help you with your work, and would be glad to share it—if you ask. At some point it will probably be worthwhile to hire the services of an *accountant.* Be sure you find one who has had experience with free-lancers and others with unconventional ways of earning money— especially important at income-tax time. The right accountant can save you a lot of time, trouble, and money— if you do your part and keep your receipts, accounts, and other documents in an orderly manner.

A balanced life: Develop respect and appreciation for *all* the dimensions of your life, and keep them in balance: physical, emotional, mental, spiritual, work, play, artistic expression, friends, family, material needs, household management, community responsibilities, pleasures, time alone, rest, meditation. When you are working for yourself it is very easy to become compulsive about the work and neglect other aspects of life.

Taking risks: By all means take risks, but not in the form of flying leaps. There are all kinds of ways to reduce the amount of risk in trying something new—many of which have been discussed in this book. And the information sources I've listed include some good advice on managing risks.

Enjoy yourself: What's the point of doing your thing instead of somebody else's if it's not fun?

13

Support Systems and Networks

No man is an Iland, intire of itselfe . . . every man is a peece of the Continent, a part of the maine. . . .
—John Donne

One of my favorite books is Robert Schrank's *Ten Thousand Working Days.** It's a delightfully told personal history of one man's working life over many years in a wide variety of occupations—plumber, farmhand, auto assembly-line worker, union organizer, sociologist, and foundation executive. The book reveals something very important about the way work is organized in our society. According to Schrank, one of the most important things that goes on in most workplaces is interpersonal interaction, socializing, or to use his favorite term for it, "schmoozing." In short, one of the main reasons people go to work every day is to talk to other people. It doesn't matter very much what the talk is about, and every office or factory has its own unique "culture."

Schrank makes it clear that this social aspect is a very important part of life for most people, and he has become

*Robert Schrank, *Ten Thousand Working Days,* Cambridge: MIT Press, 1978.

convinced that productivity on the job—any job—is directly related to the opportunity for this kind of normal social interaction. In short, people work better when they can talk to each other while they're working. There's a real need to feel part of a group, to be in on the gossip, and to have open access to useful shared information.

One of the first things a person who leaves a standard job to work autonomously discovers is that the social network is suddenly missing—unless it's just a shift from full-time to part-time work. And temporary workers rarely stay in one place long enough to be viewed as anything but outsiders. Consultants have only occasional contact with their clients, and the loneliness of the free-lance writer's work day is well documented.

This could be a real problem for people who are "working free," and it would be, except that the sort of people we have been talking about are generally pretty creative. And that creativity usually extends to finding or devising social interaction networks and support systems that serve them in the same way the ones Schrank describes serve people in offices or factories or university faculty lounges.

In fact, some of the "schmoozing" networks of creative people evolve into major institutions. Books have been written about the old gang that used to hang out at Gertrude Stein's place in Paris: Picasso, Hemingway, the Fitzgeralds, and the rest of that crowd. (See *Living Well Is the Best Revenge.**) Then there was the famous "Roundtable" group of American writers who met weekly for lunch at the Algonquin for many years.

Actors, models, and other show-biz folks have had their special tables at the Stork Club, "21," "Elaine's," or "Studio 54," where the latest issue of *Variety* could be good for half a day's worth of gossip and speculation. Artists have always

*Calvin Tompkins, *Living Well Is the Best Revenge,* New York: Avon, 1978.

managed to find each other in somebody's loft or at a favorite cafe after long hours of lonely work.

These networks are pretty well known, and serve the same important function as the office coffee break or Christmas party. Writers need a chance to get together to bitch about agents and editors; actors need each others' support when the show gets panned, and want to have somebody to celebrate with when it's coming up roses; artists need constant reassurance that their life of loneliness and poverty is really worthwhile, since very few earn a decent living from their work.

We know about these networks and support systems because we read about them in gossip columns or hear about them on TV talk shows (another support network of sorts for show-biz folk). Similar kinds of free-flowing collections of people with common experience are found in quite a few less glamorous fields.

One year when I was living in Chicago and didn't have a regular job, I started hanging out with some people who worked in restaurants. Soon my daily timetable got shifted around to mesh with theirs, and I discovered a major subculture of people who get off work at midnight, have dinner at 1:00 A.M., move on to the late music clubs till 3 or 4 A.M., and sleep till noon. Before I connected with this group, I used to wonder who all those people were who were at the beach on weekdays in the summer. Now I know. It's the "night people."

I've also discovered that science-fiction writers (and readers) gather regularly several times a year all over North America. Therapists of all sorts are constantly attending weekend workshops to get the good vibes and learn what's new in their field. There is also a huge network of just ordinary people who regularly do therapy for each other under the banner of something called "Reevaluation Counseling."

In every major city in North America and a whole lot of smaller places groups of free-lance writers gather once a month or so to hear readings of each other's work, provide friendly critiques, advice, and inside information about what magazine is looking for what kind of material, what you can expect to get paid for a 2,000-word personality profile, and other tips. Free-lance writers in fact have all kinds of support systems: summer workshops with famous writers on a hundred college campuses; *Writer's Digest* with its monthly rundown on where to sell what you write, how to present it, and a million other helpful suggestions; *Writer's Market,* the free-lancer's bible.

Once a writer has been published a few times, a different support system comes into play. It's a whole lot easier to get your work published when your submission says you've already done articles for other reputable publications. Editors need reassurance, too, and nothing works better than the information that some other editor thinks you are good.

Betsy Barley has been around in the medical writing trade for about 15 years, sometimes as a staff writer or editor, sometimes as a free-lancer. She described how the network serves her needs:

"I have a tremendous network of friends in the medical writing business. I hear about jobs and people. A lot of people are free-lancing now, so I always hear about jobs, and I hear about who's done what where. If I don't know a certain person, somebody else does." Betsy also mentioned that a good, steady connection with a man, some regular contacts with a few close friends, and frequent meditation periods are all important parts of her support system.

Some support networks are more like formal business structures. A loose collection of people in Chicago do part-time house cleaning under the umbrella of an organization called "Broom Hilda." A lady in Northampton, Massachusetts, has put together something along the same lines under the name "Rent-a-Wife." I guess if you're going to spend your days cleaning other people's houses and apartments it's a little more fun if you're part of a group.

Dorri Jacobs is one of a group of independent consultants who get together regularly in New York:

"Somebody always gives a talk at the meetings. It might be on making a sales presentation. These are all people who are doing or want to do corporate work, training, writing, technical writing, communication skills. You also make a lot of good connections at these meetings."

Chicago and several other big cities have well-organized groups of free-lance editors and writers that send a directory of their members' special skills and experience around to all the publishers in the area.

The acting game has a lot of ups and downs, and when you go for a long stretch without work it can be very depressing. Doug Werner finds it makes a big difference whom you choose to spend your spare time with:

"You can hang out with other actors and actresses who are also out of work, but that's not the best thing for your morale. It's better to be with up people." Doug makes it a point to stay close to a small group of people in his profession who have a genuine respect for each other's talents and commitment to the work. "A real good friend of mine is a cinematographer. We've shot three films together in the last year and a half, and she's excellent. She won an Academy Award for a student film she did. She's having a hard time breaking in, but I'm trying to help her, and she's helping me. She got me one job, and I turned her on to a couple of things—introduced her to some people. A girl I know who's trying to be a producer has a couple of things on the back burner. Another guy is a director and has a few things going. . . ."

Close friendships are very important to most people

who function outside traditional work structures. Michele Williams and Felicia Kaplan are good friends and help each other in a lot of different ways. If Felicia comes across some opportunity that she can't take on, or it isn't quite her thing, she may suggest Michele, and vice versa. They're also plugged into an informal network of other free-lancers of various kinds.

One good friend is all some people seem to need. Irma Wachtel:

"I am most fortunate in that a few years ago I was able to find a couple of other people who were very emotionally supportive—a woman and her husband, but mostly Eleanor. She and I are on the same wavelength. We communicate beautifully, and she is very supportive. She is her sister's keeper, and she does it magnificently. I really feel that my life would not be the same without her."

Technology does the job for some. Quite a few of the people who work at home and use computers in their work have plugged themselves into networks for what is called "computer conferencing." In this way, for example, Jeffrey Stamps in Newton, Massachusetts, can be in regular contact with people doing similar kinds of work in San Diego, Toronto, or Wickenberg, Arizona. And computer conferencing is a terrific way to get information you need for some special project or feedback on an idea from a diverse collection of thoughtful people. My friend Dennis Livingston once invited me to put a message out on the network he was on regarding a series of articles I was planning to write. I asked for people to send me any relevant information they might be able to share. A couple of weeks later I got a very interesting paper in the mail from someone on that network I'd never met. Computer conferencing people are doing that sort of thing all the time, and more and more of the people I know are getting hooked up to these networks.

We had some things to say earlier about informal education networks, Chicago's Learning Exchange, small classes taught in people's homes, and similar setups. These learning groups serve an important networking function for a lot of people and, of course, they provide those needed occasions for schmoozing.

The Society for Human Economy, one of my main ongoing projects, seems to be providing valuable support, feedback, and networking functions for a growing number of people who are trying to develop various kinds of "alternative" economic arrangements. These are people who are interested in such things as nontraditional work arrangements, simpler lifestyles, small-scale technology, conservation of energy and resources, cooperatives of various kinds, creation of well-integrated communities, economic problem solving at the local level, and the development of better economic theories and policies that reflect these values and interests. Membership chapters have been established in a number of North American cities and in several other countries, where local members help each other in all sorts of ways from barter system to starting small businesses to shared garden plots for growing some of their own food. Sometimes they get together to hear an interesting speaker, or just to socialize over a pot-luck supper.

One of the people in our local chapter said, "You know, we're all trying to do things outside the mainstream. And it's lonely and difficult sometimes to do that. The Human Economy group really helps me feel connected and not so crazy."

So far in this chapter we've been talking mostly about the sort of arrangements people make with others to overcome the feelings of isolation and loneliness that may come with "working free." But another important side to the business of making connections with other people has to do with getting work, keeping visible in the market, and getting very specific kinds of help from others when you need it. Felicia Kaplan and Michele Williams spoke of how they sometimes help each other find jobs. They're both part of a much larger network of free-lancers in Chicago—and similar groups exist in many of our larger cities. Another method Michele uses to keep expanding her contacts is to arrange to speak at conventions, where she gathers names for her mailing list:

"I did a workshop on relationships at a singles convention. When I'm planning a new workshop I'll contact those people, send out flyers, and there'll be some word of mouth. People know that I'm doing this kind of thing, so they pass my name along."

I asked Pat Lee how she finds work:

"All kinds of ways. One of the simplest, most basic things to do is to join professional organizations. I recently joined a professional women's organization. You meet other women who are doing this, that, and the other thing, who are interested in what you are doing. Being a good listener is a way of making connection. And I have a good memory. Sometimes you meet somebody and there's no real connection until a year or two later. Somebody else says to you, 'I want to do X, Y, and Z.' And you say, 'Gee, I met so-and-so and so-and-so two years ago, and they're doing this and that—give them a call.' Networking is what it's all about."

At the time I interviewed Dick Wakefield, he was preparing to leave a secure job to become a "professional networker," along with working at a part-time job. Jessica Lipnack and Jeffrey Stamps have been networking actively for years. They've become experts on how it works and have written a book* which explains in detail how many

*Jessica Lipnack and Jeffrey Stamps, *Networking—The First Report and Directory*, New York: Doubleday, 1982.

different individuals and groups do their networking, and to what end.

Jay Levinson explained how systematic networking improves his efficiency:

"I call my company Jay Levinson and Partners. The 'Partners' is the myriad of services I use. For instance, in the advertising portion of my life, to be able to service my clients I've connected up with a research person, a media buyer, a graphic artist, an announcer, musicians, a recording studio—people who do all the functions of an advertising agency. I can perform a better service for my clients if I have all these modules. Also, these people are good sources for business—I give them business, and they can return the favor.

"I also find that I don't like doing certain aspects of the business, so I delegate other people to perform those duties. In that way, I eliminate those things in my life that I don't enjoy, with the result that almost everything I do is a task that I look forward to."

Charles Mitts runs a small free-lance advertising business in Chicago. Charlie's networking includes some very effective *bartering*. For example, he might arrange a trade between a radio station and a restaurant—some free air time for an ad in exchange for a few free dinners—and charge an appropriate fee for putting the exchange together.

The life of a free-lancer need not mean being cut off from valuable institutional supports of various kinds. I do my work in a community that includes a major university and four other colleges—five excellent libraries, lots of opportunities for contacts with people with many different interests and skills, and, because of the intense competition for business, the lowest prices for photocopying anywhere!

Another major advantage of doing one's work near a

university of that word-of-mouth recommendations are passed around widely in such communities. So if you happen to be a good free-lance editor, for example, it's going to be relatively easy to find plenty of work. Same for a free-lance accountant, word-processing specialist, child-care person, psychotherapist, or whatever your specialty might be.

And while we're on the subject of college towns, it's worth mentioning that colleges and universities have been more accepting than most other kinds of organizations of the concept of job sharing, which might be viewed as a unique sort of two-person mutual support system.

Many people view the entertainment business as one of the most insecure fields a person could choose for earning a living. It certainly can be, but offsetting the big risk of never getting hired is the fact that the industry is totally unionized. This means that once you do get hired for a job, there are all sorts of guarantees. Andy Federman explained how it works for film editors:

"We have contracts. So there are certain rights that are guaranteed to all free-lancers. Anytime you work on a film you automatically get a lot of rights (overtime pay rates, for example), and you're covered with a pension, welfare, and other benefits."

These union arrangements apply as well to actors, musicians, stagehands, camera operators—virtually everybody in the business.

In summary, "working free" does not have to be a lonely life. There is a way to make useful connections, and there are sources of help for solving problems in almost every field. You have to know where to look for them. I've identified a few and provided some information about them at the back of the book.

14

Some Enlightened Employers

. . . the people who work for you today have different aspirations and ambitions and, in some ways, are brighter than before. You must be more open, more candid, more participatory with these people. That requires a different style of management. You can't be as authoritarian. You have to be more sensitive, more aware.

—William Agee
President, Bendix Corporation

Although this book has so far been essentially devoted to people who have found a way to work on their own terms outside established institutions, we must not forget that the large majority of working people will continue to report to a boss in one way or another. Does this mean that they are all going to have to settle for a life of rigid bureaucratic routines? I think not. At least some people who work for someone else on a more or less regular basis have found that employers can be sensitive to an individual's special needs and preferences.

In other words there are some employers who put performance of the task well ahead of such concerns as where the employee happens to be at a particular time. And the accumulating research on flexible work arrangements indicates that these employers are coming out well ahead on such things as productivity levels, quality of the work done, reductions of lost work time, and general employee morale.

To put the matter another way, "enlightened" employers tend to attract better people to work for them. And as a result, they often find that they can spend much less time "managing" people—time that can be devoted to more important things.

What constitutes an "enlightened" employer? The general criterion is someone who has real respect for the people who do the work, whether that work be complicated management decisions or the most routine daily tasks. But in the context of this book we can be more specific. Given that a lot of people would like greater control over how they spend their own time even though they need to work to earn a living, it is reasonable to suggest that the model employer is one who recognizes fully that different people have different dimensions to their lives, and that the work can get done without forcing employees into rigid time boxes.

What are the possibilities? Several years ago the National Council on Alternative Work Patterns did a survey on a large and diverse group of employers including business firms and government and educational institutions to determine to what extent flexible work options were available at that time. Their work resulted in a directory listing 235 organizations that had implemented—at some level— one of the following: flextime, permanent part-time jobs, job sharing, or a reduced work week. Browsing through this document, one can begin to get a feel for relative degrees of enlightenment. At one end of the scale is an employer that offers permanent part-time work, but to only four employees. At the other is a firm like Hewlett-

Packard, which has implemented all the options listed for significant numbers of its employees and is committed to making it work. That is very important, since some employers will give a half-hearted nod toward one of these things as "an experiment" and then make sure it doesn't work. Such an employer can, of course, claim, "We tried that, but it didn't work out."

Also, some changes are more adventurous (and usually offer the employee more flexibility) than others. Control Data Corporation and the Continental Illinois National Bank & Trust Co. of Chicago have gone to special efforts to make it possible for some of their employees to work in their homes, in the former case, with a particular emphasis on enabling physically handicapped people to perform responsible jobs with a minimum of personal inconvenience. The Ford Foundation recently announced a new policy of granting paid leave time to new fathers, while we must remember that at the other end of that spectrum are the thousands of new mothers whose decision as to whether or not to have a child still involves a major issue of job security.

It may be worth pointing out that flexible work options have been common practice for many years in a number of European private and public institutions. Sweden even has a comprehensive public law on conditions of employment, which specifies that all employees must be eligible for flexible working hours, leave time for parenting, part-time work, and other arrangements that make for a healthier integration of work and the rest of one's life.

Why is North America so far behind Europe on these matters? Are we in fact so far behind? What is being done on our side? If we look only at official documentation on flexible work options, we're still in the Dark Ages. But there may be reason to question the "official" picture. We may be doing a little better than the numbers tell us. A couple of experiences I had while interviewing for this book are suggestive.

On one occasion I was visiting with a neighbor just prior to a trip to Washington, D.C. She asked the reason for my trip, and I said, "I've heard that there are a number of new experiments in job sharing around Washington." I was just about to explain to her what "job sharing" is when she said, "Oh, that's what I do. I share a secretarial job at a construction firm with another woman. It really works out great. I like to work, but I also want to have time with my kids while they are still around." Diane Stuhrcke had been sharing this job for a couple of years, and no one had ever made a big thing of it.

On another occasion I was talking with Michele Williams about the range of things I wanted to be sure to cover in this book, and she said, "Oh. You should talk to my mother. She works for a small company and they've just given her a year off with full pay. They've started doing that with all the people who have been with them for a long time."

I began to realize that like most people who research the world of work, I was inclined to focus on the big companies or the big government organizations, because whenever one of them does something unusual that the public might think well of, the public relations department makes sure people hear about it. As I reflected on all this I realized that there must be thousands of small organizations deserving to be called "enlightened employers." Without any fanfare, they operate routinely on the principle of making the work fit the person instead of the other way around.*

*I have a continuing interest in keeping track of developments in the area of flexible and autonomous work arrangements and would be particularly interested in hearing from small business firms or other organizations that permit their employees to work out their own time arrangements in unconventional ways.

Another cause for optimism is emerging. Over the past few years a number of prominent work organizations have made it known that they were embarking on programs of flexible work arrangements. All New York City employees, for example, came under such a new arrangement in 1980. When these big employers make such an announcement, an instant response comes in from many other employers who apparently have been considering such changes and seek information on specifics and reassurances that it can be done. Paul Dickson described the phenomenon in his book *The Future of the Workplace.**

"Executives from several firms which had converted their operations to new time arrangements like the 4-day work week and the flexible work day tell of having to resort to form responses to be sent out to the hundreds of other companies that want information on what they have done and with what result."

People who prefer a better balance between work and the other things in their lives are apparently being listened to. And as more and more big projects like the state of Wisconsin's "Project Join," in which 150 people share 75 jobs, mature and are analyzed for results, the evidence mounts that a diversity of work schedules pays off for employers. "Enlightened" employers are turning out to be satisfied employers.

Forbes and Wagner, an electronic-component assembly plant in Silver Creek, New York, circulated a questionnaire about preferred work time among its employees and found that about 20 percent of the people wanted to work fewer hours. Hours were subsequently reduced for many of these people, and according to plant manager Norm Sager, people now working a 6-hour day are generally producing as much as, and in some cases more than, those

*Paul Dickson, *The Future of the Workplace,* New York: Weybright & Talley, 1975.

working an 8-hour day. Attendance has improved, and employee morale is up.

That item came from the "Newsletter of the National Council for Alternative Work Patterns," and Gail Rosenberg and Maureen McCarthy, the entrepreneurs who created that important information network, have recently published a book* documenting similar results among a wide variety of employers.

The pattern is clear. Flexible work arrangements can bring increased efficiency and other advantages to many employers. But the rewards to an employer can also be very personal in some circumstances. Rowlie Sylvester ran several manufacturing companies for a number of years. Since he's something of a "free spirit" I was curious about how he functioned in the role of company president, so I asked him about his relationship with his employees at that time:

"Well, first of all, they all owned stock in the business, and I ended up selling out to them, which gave me a nice way out. I never told anybody much what to do. I liked the arrangement where I could do the kind of work that I enjoyed most, which was inventing and product development, and then selling my own inventions. I was happy enough if they would take over the rest of it and run it. If somebody was going to do a job, I wasn't going to tell them how to do it. It was pretty much each person running their own activities and their own life, and setting their own hours—within limits. We all worked reasonably hard when we worked, and we all took quite a bit of time off. Then we split up the profits at the end of the year in a way . . . I always took the biggest share."

The last line was delivered with a big laugh. Rowlie seems to have a special capacity for enjoying life, whatever

*Maureen E. McCarthy and Gail S. Rosenberg, *Work Sharing Case Studies*, Kalamazoo, Mich.: The W. E. Upjohn Institute for Employment Research, 1981.

role he may be functioning in at the moment. And let's face it, it's probably a lot harder to pull that off at Exxon or IBM.

Another of these "enlightened" small businessmen is Roy Moss, who a few years ago moved his pewter engraving company from the New York suburbs to a tiny country town in upstate New York. His entire operation, grossing a quarter of a million dollars a year with sales all over the country, is now housed in a lovely old farmhouse surrounded by the spectacular scenery of New York's Washington County. During what other business firms would call coffee breaks, Moss encourages his employees to go cross-country skiing or do yoga or play frisbee on the surrounding acreage. He says, "My people are aware of cost controls and expected dollar-per-hour productivity, and prefer to work at 'above acceptable' productivity levels. They can make their own hours as long as the work gets done, and done well."

Sounds like good management.

Sometimes employees are so conditioned to meaningless routines that they have real difficulty when the opportunity for greater flexibility is made available. Back in the early 1970s, Ted Peacock left the world of the big corporation to set up his own small book publishing company. I remember a conversation with him about one year after he started.

"I told my people right from the start that there were tasks that needed to get done, but I didn't especially care what formal work hours were kept. It was O.K. with me if people wanted to do some of their work at home instead of in the office, or whatever—as long as the work got done when we needed it. And if some people really had nothing to do, I would tell them to take the rest of the day off—to make that decision on their own and not feel they had to ask me for permission. It took about six months for some of my people to realize that I was serious about it. Frankly it makes me nervous having people fiddling around in the office when they don't really have anything to do. Sometimes there just isn't enough work to go around, and it doesn't seem right to penalize people for that."

Employers like Ted may not be the majority, but they're all over the place. It's worth remembering that most employers are decent folks, and it's quite possible that no one ever brought up the idea of flexible work options in a serious way with them. So there are two different strategies to consider in trying to connect with a work situation that suits your special needs. One is to do a careful search for employers who are already "enlightened." The other is to do a first-class selling job on your present boss, or the one you want to go to work for. In either case you can get some help from the various consultants, organizations, and books listed at the end of the book.

A good place to start is the *Directory* of the National Council for Alternative Work Patterns. If your local library doesn't have a copy, urge them to get it. It's a browse-through book that will tell you whether any employers in your area have already implemented flexible work options. If not, it will at least give you some confidence that the idea is not so far out. You'll get a picture of what a lot of other people are doing.

The next step is to take some personal initiative. One strategy that I particularly like is to call up a place that interests you and tell the personnel manager, or, better yet, the president if you can get to that person, "I'm doing research for a magazine article on flexible work arrangements and would like to know what policies your organization has in effect with regard to such things as flextime, permanent part-time jobs, job sharing, paid leave time, provisions for people to work at home, or other arrangements." Probably one employer out of ten will have something concrete to say of a positive nature, but you may pick up some clues as to whether a given company would even be open to considering such things, especially if you are talking to the president. The whole exercise will be a consciousness raiser on this subject for everyone involved. You can be sure that the person on the other end of that phone will think more than once in the ensuing days, "I wonder how it would work out if we tried something like that?" You may even turn up a couple of employers who are already having the usual success with one or more of these arrangements, and of course that's the place to go looking for your job.

In case the whole exercise leaves you with still no good leads, you can at least pay for your time and effort by selling a story on "Innovations in Flexible Work Arrangements" to your local newspaper, even if the "story" says "Look what they're doing all over the country but not here."

The other option is to become as knowledgeable as you possibly can about the sort of time arrangement you particularly want, read all the books, gather good documentation on several other employers similar to the one you have in mind who have successfully implemented job sharing or whatever, and go sell the boss on the idea, casting yourself in the role of the ideal person to make this thing work. In short, do your homework well, and make a very confident, well-documented presentation as to how it will benefit the *employer* very specifically. You may be surprised at the result, especially if you listen carefully to the possible problems the boss raises and give very good answers to those objections.

I am not describing a personal fantasy here. This procedure has been highly developed over the past few years by a group called "New Ways to Work" in California and by a few other consultants around the country with good results. There are quite a few companies and other organizations that got talked into something like job sharing in just this way, and are now pleased as can be with the way it has worked out.

Employers want to be good managers. They want efficiency, productivity, good employee morale. And they want to eliminate excessive absenteeism. More and more of them are learning that flexible work arrangements are a good way to achieve those goals.

15

A Modest Proposal for a Rational System of Allocating Work

Every one of us has the responsibility and the capability to construct his or her own map of reality and to dream, think, and act on the basis of it. . . .

—E. F. Schumacher and
Peter Gillingham
Good Work

In his book *The Zero-Sum Society*,* MIT economist Lester Thurow, wrestling with the seemingly intractable problems of our economic system, says at one point, "We cannot ration work."

The fact is that "we," whoever that is, have already rationed worked. Some people get all the work they need. Some get more than their share, and many others get none. Some get paid for their work and some do not. Certain kinds of work have been reserved for those fortunate enough to get to go to Harvard or Yale. Other kinds of work have been essentially reserved for people with

*Lester Thurow, *The Zero-Sum Society*, New York: Basic Books, 1980.

171

black skin. Some work has traditionally been "women's work." It is not a question of whether we can ration work, but whether we can ration it in a more equitable way. And now that some of these old ways of allocating work are beginning to break down, why not use some imagination, and devise a rational scheme? We can, if enough of us insist on it. But it will take some imagination and a great deal of education to redistribute work in our society, even though the benefits of doing so may be quite obvious.

What form might the redistribution of work take? There are many possibilities, many variations.

Just as there are various ways of organizing and allocating work, there are different ways to arrange not to work. One way is called a vacation. In academia, and a very tiny segment of the corporate world, there are sabbaticals—a whole year off with pay. Then there are layoffs and firings—another way of keeping people from working. Some of the more subtle methods include having the jobs located so far from where people live that they cannot afford to get to where the work is. (A recent article in *The New York Times* told of a restaurant in posh Westchester County that had to close off some of its space because there were no poor people in the immediate area of the sort who would ordinarily take jobs as bus boys or dishwashers.) Another less obvious way work gets rationed is the constant setting up of only one kind of choice for people who want to work: 40 hours a week, 50 weeks a year, or nothing. This system would be the easiest to change.

If we really wanted to achieve a better distribution of work—an arrangement that would improve the quality of people's lives, reduce absenteeism, increase productivity and creativity at work, and strengthen family life—we could do it. There are so many possible ways to go about it that it is difficult to know where to start. Let me propose

one possible model, not necessarily as the best possible
solution, but to help us think more clearly about the possibilities. I start with two assumptions:

1. Most adults want or need to work to earn income during a large part of their lives.
2. Most adults will inevitably spend some substantial
   blocks of time not working for pay.

Now let us look for a moment at the usual patterns of
work time and non-work time. The usual pattern for the
majority of white males has been to enter the paid workforce anywhere from age 16 to 20, to continue working for
pay, with time out each year for vacations—in most cases
not more than a month—and then stop working at age 65.

The usual pattern for some other people is to be unable
to find paid work for long periods of time, so that earning
a living is a matter of intense pressure and great insecurity
for much of their lives.

The usual pattern for women who chose to raise children is to work for pay for a few years, then work without
pay for a few years while the children are young, and then
go back into the paid workforce, unless, of course, they
can't find a job.

Obviously, many variations are possible on these "usual"
patterns, including the variant of black males who, because
of our present system of rationing work, may reach their
mid-twenties without ever having had the experience of
doing work that provides income.

We must realize that this whole messy "system" is simply
arbitrary. It's something that evolved without anybody really thinking carefully about it, let alone planning it. The
U.S. and Canadian governments have long had a Department of Labor, but the thousands of people who work
there have never been charged with the task of proposing
strategies for major reorganization of our work-rationing

system. Several hundred "task forces" and conferences on the subject of work haven't really addressed this possibility. The reason? My best guess is that old assumptions about social organization are just too comfortable, even when they are wrong. To propose something genuinely new is just too threatening to too many people. Nonetheless, I'm proposing a major change, because I believe the conflict between groups in our society will soon be uncontrollable if we don't. Also because too many people are unhappy, while something concrete could be done to improve their lives.

What I am proposing here will seem much too simple to many readers. I know perfectly well that whatever new work-rationing system we might devise will be full of unpredictable complexities. And that is fine, because otherwise all those people at the Department of Labor would have nothing to do and would soon be unemployed.

Let us then consider what follows simply as a concept to be embellished by others. Remember that it is only one of many possibilities.* We'll call it Applegath's Plan for the Rational Distribution of Work.

We begin by assuming that at any given time there is a relatively fixed amount of work in society which must be done. If we stick with old formulas for the moment, we might say there are 110 million jobs in the American economy—including unfilled jobs and combinations of part-time jobs to make full-time equivalents. There are also a fixed number of adults who want or need to work to earn money. Some of these people would prefer to work 50 hours a week every week of the year without a break.

---

*I am not the first to propose an alternative plan for the rationing of work. Carlos Varsavsky's "Continuous Work Week" (New York: Institute for Economic Analysis, New York University, 1979) is an excellent contribution to the subject. I would be pleased if the publication of my own book resulted in the generation of many more possible schemes.

Others would like to work only in the mornings. Some others would like to work nine months out of each year. And some would like to be able to move in and out of the job market as they need or do not need money. Very likely there will always be a very small group who, for whatever reasons, choose not to work for pay at all—housewives, some artists, some people with inherited wealth, and people with serious mental or physical health problems.

Out of these diverse needs we can see a spectrum: the workaholic at one end, and the person of leisure at the other. Given the resources available to North Americans, no reason exists why every one of these people cannot be accommodated, as long as we are willing to step out of some old ruts.

For example, if some people insist on working all the time, they should be perfectly free to do so. But whether they should be *paid* for *all* the time they work is a question that has two possible answers, not just one. Why should we over-reward people with a *pathological* attachment to work, while we under-reward the millions of housewives and others who do a great deal of hard work for which they never get paid?

At the other end of the spectrum, any country that has enough resources to keep on building nuclear bombs when it already has enough of those to destroy the world, certainly has enough resources to keep people alive at some modest material level whether they choose to do what someone else defines as "work" or not.

So far, then, I am proposing that our new work rationing system have some outside limits: there is a point beyond which we will not continue paying people no matter how much work they do; and we will not let anyone starve.

Within these limits life becomes much more interesting. Let's see how we can change the pattern of unemployment, always a severe problem. There *appears* not to be enough work to go around. The employment statistics are visible daily. What is not visible is an accurate count (or even a rough guess) of the number of people who would be delighted to stop working—to trade income for leisure—for two days a week, or three months a year, or one year out of five—as long as they would be guaranteed a subsistence wage for the period out of the workforce. If we allowed these people a "free market" for their labor—that is, if we allowed them to *not* work when they do not need or want to—we would find that there is some work for the currently unemployed, though perhaps not what we usually think of as full-time jobs.

So a lot of arrangements about work time will have to be changed, and, of course, managers will have to manage differently. But aren't managers paid to be good at managing? One test of their ability is whether they can deal effectively with change itself. Surely managers in those organizations that have already implemented flexible work options are not innately superior to all other managers. Good people usually rise to meet the demands made on them, especially when they understand the benefits.

What about the benefits?

If we had a planned rationing of work instead of the present chaos (which some economists charmingly mistake for a labor "market"), the mental health of all the people would improve dramatically. The costs of illness, crime, alcoholism, and drug addiction, among other things, would begin to go down, and the people we see on our streets would look happier, more relaxed.

Why? Very simply because they would each be able to *plan* a *balanced* life for themselves, knowing *in advance* when they would be working for pay and when they would not. Contrast that with the present arrangement, under which so many people are either unable to find paid work or are working when they'd rather not be.

As I write this, I can "feel" the agitation of my potential critics. Some might say, "You can't expect an untrained person to step into a manager's job." Perhaps not, but there would be no need to, since there are so many unemployed or underemployed people around who could handle most mid-level management tasks. In fact, new people with fresh perspectives might even solve some of the old problems!

Another possible objection: "How do you expect an executive earning $80,000 a year to suddenly live for a year on $20,000? An executive earning that kind of money should be presumed to be a good manager. A good manager who *knows* five years in advance that he will have a year of unusually low income could provide for it in advance, unlike the man who is suddenly "let go" at age 54.

The sort of transition I propose would not be *easy*. It might not even work. But does our present system work? Are we making good progress toward solving our problems?

We have a choice. We can devote ourselves to finding the holes in Applegath's Plan, dismissing it and other plans that require major changes as utopian. Or we could devote some of our energy through the 1980s to a serious reconsideration of the issue raised here, calling for ideas and plans from anyone who can think creatively about the place of work in our lives.

In short, we can choose to be "conservative"— preserving and patching up a system of work allocation devised 200 years ago—or we can make the best possible use of our imagination, our experience, and our knowledge to make life a whole lot better for everyone.

16

A Scenario for Work in the Future

The task is not easy. In the past, enjoyment of the few has always been achieved at the expense of drudgery for the masses. This we cannot afford any longer—not just ethically, but practically as well. The power of the disadvantaged is great enough to destroy the world, if not to heal it. Therefore we must find solutions that will lift as many people as possible into a pattern of growth.

—Mihaly Csikszentmihalyi
Beyond Boredom and Anxiety

No one can predict the future, but developments always occur in the present that point the way to some aspects of the future which can either be developed further or ignored. In short, to some extent we can create for ourselves the sort of future we want.

Usually some particularly creative or perceptive individual comes up with a vision of how the future might be better than the present in some specific ways, and then sets about campaigning hard to sell that vision to the rest of us. In the United States the process is ritualized in presidential elections, but it has been happening throughout history with people as diverse as Jesus Christ and Henry Ford.

178

Without presuming to be in a class with these prominent historical figures, I hereby announce that I see the possibility of some better ways to get work done in our society, ways that will improve the quality of life for most people while maintaining a high level of productivity and encouraging much more creative innovation than we are used to seeing. Anyone who has read this far already has the drift of my vision. In this chapter I hope to pull it all together, to make the picture more coherent, and to actively campaign on behalf of the "alternative future" I would like to see in the world of work.

Actually, I am certain that my preferred alternative future will come about. It will be *one* of the ways work gets organized. The important question is, will enough people in positions of decision-making responsibility see the benefits of flexible, more autonomous work arrangements to have it become the dominant mode within the next 20 or 30 years, or will such practices remain the good fortune of relatively few?

Despite the fact that most people will almost certainly continue to do their work under the old bureaucratic routines for some years to come, I am willing to predict a quiet, gradual change. My prediction rests on three premises:

1. More and more individuals are becoming determined to find ways of working that fit their own priorities and preferences, whether by inventing their own jobs, changing career fields, finding employers who will give them the flexibility and autonomy they want, or selling current employers on the advantages of alternative work arrangements.

2. The number of employers who are offering employees such options as permanent part-time jobs with significant responsbility, flexible working hours, job sharing, and paid leave time for various purposes is constantly

growing. Once employers take flexible work options seriously, they tend to be so pleased with the results that they wouldn't consider going back to the rigidities of the old system. With the continuing pressure for such options from women's organizations combined with the steady publicity evolving on the subject the idea will gain in popularity and more and more organizations will give it a try.

3. (This is the clincher.) It is very clear that once a person finds a way to earn a decent living on his or her own terms, there is usually no reversion to the old way, except in the case of major personal emergencies.

These, then, are the primary reasons for my optimism about the future of work. But some other factors are worth mentioning. One of the important ones is that the kinds of changes we have been discussing here are often simply more *convenient*. After all, in an age when information of incredible complexity is stored in computers with the possibility of instant retrieval or manipulation by a terminal that can be in any chosen location, why should a person whose job is to process information (financial analyst, secretary, editor, accountant, broker) go to all the trouble of spending an hour or two fighting the traffic every day to show up at the head office? Or, if an employer has two very competent people both putting their best into one job, why would that employer ever want to go back to having only one person in that position? If a salesman on the road can be trusted to perform well without daily supervision, why not hire people like that for all the other jobs in the company, instead of maintaining all the headaches that go with "managing" people all day long?

My suggested newer ways of organizing work have an added advantage in that they tend to dramatically *increase efficiency*. The studies which have been done on job sharing show that when you hire two people for one job, you typically get the work output of something like one and a half people—for the price of one. And it has long been known that people work better when they feel good, when they are not frustrated, when their lives are well integrated. So an employer who is smart enough to take into account some of the other factors in an employee's life in arranging the work schedule is going to get more efficient time on the job.

We have been talking mostly about the prospects for change in traditional work organizations here, but what are the prospects for all those people who want to be free-lancers or consultants, or who want to combine five different kinds of work? Well-organized, competent, independent operators have a very bright future indeed. For some years managers have been finding ways to get important work done without putting more people on the payroll. The advantages of hiring an independent entrepreneur for a one-shot job are clear: no fringe benefits to be paid, no need for office space for a manager and a secretary. No personnel policies to worry about. Just tell Ms. Wilson of Wilson Associates what it is you want and when you want it, work out the financial arrangements, and sit back and wait for the final report to appear on your desk. And, speaking of efficiency, if Beverly Wilson doesn't deliver top quality on time at the right price, you don't use her again. There are 20 other good people doing that kind of work on a free-lance basis.

The U.S. government employs thousands of consultants. Every new administration makes noises about getting rid of some of them, but government is a complicated business and the bureaucracies get so tangled up that there will always be a need to hire an independent consultant to get something done efficiently. And that's not just in Washington. The same problems exist in Ottawa, New York State, Los Angeles County, and the province of Quebec. In short, government at all levels will always be a good market for consultants and will increasingly become a place to find flexible jobs on the payroll.

We've mentioned that the entertainment industry is almost totally dependent on free-lancers, and with the explosion of cable-TV programming, more opportunities for all kinds of talent, including good independent management talent, will be available. Some of the big money in cable TV is being made by independent program packagers.

Something similar has been going on in the book-publishing business. Many people think book publishers do everything in-house including the actual printing and binding of books. The day when that was true is long gone. For many years book publishing has been a kind of brokerage business between authors, agents, editors, typesetters, printers, warehousing, and shipping operations. Independent entrepreneurs have found profitable niches all over this business, from free-lance editors and agents who work at home to free-lance book designers or proofreaders or indexers. Small firms are set up just to do warehousing and shipping for several smaller publishers. Book "packagers" develop a concept for a book, find the author, and may go as far as developing the publicity package, while the "publisher" performs only the routine functions. Book publishing has become a highly decentralized business, and could become even more so. One of these days, major New York publishers will discover that most of their people could do their work just as well at much less cost somewhere outside their exhorbitantly expensive Manhattan office space.

The pattern of decentralization, spinning off different functions to independent operators, that characterizes the book-publishing industry will very likely be followed by the television industry, and as managers in other fields watch the results, they will ask themselves more and more where they can find a sharp entrepreneur to take over a special market, or a corporate communications project, or whatever.

There will be readers who will say, "All this may be very good when the economy is booming, but in hard times people want job security." My answer is that people think of security in different ways, and they will arrange their lives in the way that works best for them. Let me remind the skeptics that those who seek security in a job with a big corporation may be among the ones laid off when a plant has to be closed down or whenever the profit margin starts to shrink significantly.

On the other hand, many people just don't believe there is such a thing as security. Certainly many of the people interviewed in this book feel that way. Such people make it their business to be constantly aware of special opportunities, constantly developing and refining their talents and skills, constantly taking manageable risks. These people also have greater personal flexibility. They tend not to be locked in to some fixed salary level. They are used to making changes in their material standard of living without becoming traumatized. Often for such people, difficult economic circumstances stimulate increased creativity and productivity.

Hard times, when they come, affect all of us. Which group of people will weather severe economic difficulties better? Out of which group will the truly creative new approaches emerge that will be necessary to reconstruct a devastated economic system? What does "security" mean in this context?

In my work with the Human Economy Center, I have found that posing the prospect of a major economic collapse is an excellent way to get people to think creatively about what sort of alternative future they might wish to invest their time and effort in helping to bring about. It is not important whether people believe it is actually going to happen. It provides a sort of "clean slate" for building a new vision. With regard to the reorganization of work, perhaps the following "alternative vision" could move us significantly toward that improvement in equality of life most North Americans seem to be yearning for.

In the chapter "Work and the Rest of your Life" I emphasized the place of learning in a person's life and touched on the relationship between formal education and the kinds of work people do. Education is a good place to start to build our alternative future scenario, because if we pay careful attention to what goes on in our present formal learning system we discover that in the course of teaching different kinds of things—information and skills, and habits and attitudes—it prepares us at ever earlier ages to become specialists. A specialist is excessively dependent on others for everything that is not her or his particular specialty. One result is that in a society in which nearly everyone is dependent on automobiles for transportation and typewriters or word-processors for conveying information, only a small minority of the population knows how to adjust a carburetor or replace a head gasket, and most people cannot type efficiently. We have become accustomed to depending on other specialists for our most fundamental needs, and certainly for all kinds of service.

We also learn to be competitive; and people who are conditioned to always see themselves as competing with others will go through life missing out on the enhanced efficiencies and pleasures that come with cooperation and sharing.

Work will take its proper place in the social order again only when people learn at an early age to be relatively self-reliant, competent in a wide variety of basic life skills, confident enough to take some risks, well trained in the differences between reasonable risks and foolish ones, and capable of working in cooperation with others.

It would be good if the formal channels of education could help to develop some understanding of what constitutes a balanced and satisfying life. As a person learns about the essentials of life in such a curriculum, various opportunities should be provided for young people to try out real-life responsibilities. (We could call some of these opportunities "work," but it would be better if we didn't start early in life to set work apart from everything else.) An important feature of the system at this stage would be the opportunity to make mistakes and to learn from them without penalties, emotional or otherwise.

Thus, I could envision a typical 12-year-old of either sex having gained some good experience at such fundamental life requirements as child care, use of a typewriter and computer console, some simple budgeting of funds, preparation of an income-tax form, and some of the basics of auto mechanics and bicycle repair. Depending on how good the learning system is, the child may well have the experience of growing some of the family's food, doing some household repairs, running some very small business, teaching other children, mastering the use of a library.

As "education" progresses, in addition to learning the basics of language and communication, math, sciences, and the fine arts, and having regular, meaningful occasions for testing and refining those skills, the student would begin to learn such essential skills as how to make intelligent decisions, how to manage risk, how to evaluate personal performance in various areas, how to learn from mistakes, how to successfully integrate feelings and rational processes—in short, the fundamental skills for survival in a complex society.

As this educational process develops, a progressively greater integration of what we have traditionally called education and work evolves. A 19-year-old might be expected to have had thorough exposure to and some degree of responsibility for at least a dozen different kinds of real-world tasks from house cleaning to selling classified ads in a newspaper to handling an important part of some scientific experiment.

Gradually the person involved in this process (we can thankfully now eliminate the demeaning social label "student") will be given more and more feedback on the kinds of things she or he does particularly well, and will be encouraged to spend more time and effort on those things that hold greatest interest. And as always, throughout the process, there is the expectation that the person will take ample time for reflection, relaxation, physical exercise, and socializing, to keep life in balance.

It would be fun to spell out more details of this new curriculum for progressing from dependent childhood to self-confident adulthood, but it is not necessary here. I think I have probably made my point as to what is missing from our present arrangements for "education."

I will emphasize one point again, because it is such a major departure from the way we do things now. That is the necessity of a constant integration of "work" and learning that is to continue throughout a person's life. This must be arranged in such a way that in the process of maturing, a person develops the capability for self-education in any area of choice, while at the same time reducing the dependence on outside institutional structures. (A good friend of mine left the ministry to go into the business of developing small-scale hydropower sites. In one year, Peter Schneider taught himself an enormous amount about business finance, planning, and engineering without ever stepping into a classroom.)

If you now reflect for a while on some of the conse-
quences of only the first part of my future scenario, you
will find that the world begins to look quite different. For
example, at what point in such a system would it be decided that some forms of work should receive payment
while other forms do not? At what point would certain
people come to view themselves as "bosses" and others as
"employees"? In fact, the lines would be pretty fuzzy from
the start and would be likely to stay that way. Meanwhile
society would be transformed from large collections of
passive, dependent people playing out boring bureaucratic roles within rigid structures to self-motivated people
building and shaping a world they could enjoy.

We don't have to go for the whole scenario. Any
significant move in the direction proposed would make a
big difference in the quality of our lives.

Now, having gotten our people through the early years
of life and properly educated, how do we organize the
work that needs to be done?

Step one is to find out how much actual work exists that
is really necessary, and finally admit to ourselves that there
is simply not enough real work to keep everybody who
wants to work outside the home fully engaged for 40
hours a week, 52 weeks a year, without a break, from age
21 or so until 65 or 70. The evidence for this assertion is
clear enough. We have always had some substantial level
of unemployment, but we have never dealt with it in the
most rational, equitable way. The rational way would be to
carefully parcel out the available work so that everyone
who wants to work and needs income can do so.

Specifically, I would propose a system along the following lines. Begin by changing the norm, the thing most
people do, from standard, full-time jobs to smaller segments. These segments might be shorter work weeks,
shorter days, shorter years, but the system would be or-

ganized so that everyone who needs paid work would get at least the equivalent of nine months of full-time work each year, unless less was wanted (instead of nine months of full-time it might be twelve months of four-day weeks or three-day weeks or whatever). One of the many benefits of this plan, aside from the obvious one of parents having more time with their families, is that everyone would have a little more of that precious leisure time that is so necessary for human creativity. The relationship between leisure and creativity has been articulated by most of our great geniuses in every field of endeavor, and if we want more of the latter, we must have more of the former.

A recurrent theme in the American business press in recent years has been a perceived lack of innovation, new ideas, new approaches, new processes, and new forms of organization, especially in comparison with the Japanese. Innovation is creativity, and creativity requires some reasonable lesure. Keeping your nose to the grindstone just means you keep going in the old ruts. Great leaps forward in knowledge occur when people have time to step back for a while and study the big picture. Why not institutionalize some reasonable degree of leisure as a necessary condition of the "quality of life" for everyone?

How will all the work get done? More joyfully. And certainly more efficiently. Ask yourself honestly how often you have observed yourself or someone else proving Parkinson's famous law (work expands to fill the time available), making a small job last till quitting time?

Now there are those poor neurotics who are incapable of enjoying leisure, the workaholics. We should simply recognize that disease for what it is and stop paying those people premium wages for their affliction. Let them work as much as they like, so long as it doesn't deprive some other person of useful work, and as long as they don't expect to receive more money than more balanced people.

Does this begin to sound like a rejection of the traditional work ethic? Of course it is. And since a majority of people respond to opinion polls these days saying that "quality of life" is more important than making a lot of money, perhaps it is time to incorporate that awesome change in North American values into our work systems at all levels.

But we need not be rigid about how we reorganize work. Once we confront the real shortage of meaningful work and decide to give people what they want most in life, we can find all sorts of possible ways of going about it. Another possible variation would be to reserve "full-time" jobs for people between the ages of 30 and 55 who have responsibiities for the financial support of others besides themselves, with everyone else given enough work to earn a decent living. Perhaps under either plan there could be an exception to the rules for people who create their own jobs.

Flexibility would be the guiding principle. Anything that would prevent the recurrence of the present arrangement, where too many people work all the time, sacrificing too much of the rest of their lives to the office clock, while others are deprived totally from earning a living.

The flexibility I am suggesting as a general policy could soften the difficulties for people in bad economic times as well. When the economy is shrinking, we would reduce everyone's work time (in labor union circles it's called "work sharing"), rather than putting some people out of work completely while others get to retain full-time jobs.

And what happens to our older people under the proposed new arrangement? It is hoped something better than the present system where a person is "on the job" five days a week for 40 or 50 years with very little time free for other interests, then is suddenly confronted with nothing but free time. No one in our present system is much surprised at the very large number of people who die soon after retirement. Putting people out to pasture with no skills for the constructive use of leisure after years of routine work is actually a rather cruel social device, one we could well do without.

In contrast, the alternative work scenario proposed would encourage people throughout their lifetimes to be always engaged in learning and developing new interests and skills. And most important, they would have the *time* for these pursuits and the common experience of integrating them with the demands of the normal job. Further, in a society that saw no special advantage in rigid work weeks and work years, a person could gradually reduce the number of days and hours worked per year or per week, spending gradually increasing amounts of time on volunteer work in the community, artistic pursuits, learning, travel, or whatever gives the individual the most satisfaction.

When people who have continued to grow all their lives grow old, they are a lot more interesting, a lot more fun to have around, a lot more useful to the community and family than old people who have been in the same narrow rut for years. Perhaps we could break the nasty habit of shoving our elders off out of sight into those dreadful prisons called "nursing homes."

Utopian Vision or Plain Old Social Change?

Readers will respond to my proposal for an alternative future in their own ways. Some will see it as pie in the sky, totally impractical, unrealistic. Others may see it as an ideal well worth working toward. Perhaps some will share my own view that our society is changing in many different ways, and very rapidly, and that my scenario points the general *direction* in which we might go to make our work systems more *equitable* (a notion once highly favored in democratic societies). After all, awesome changes are taking place in the sciences and technology, in the knowledge available to us, and in social institutions as basic as the family. Why should we remain mired in a 200-year-old concept of how to organize the work of society, while physicists and evolution theorists change our fundamental picture of reality almost daily?

The most important question, of course, is, will it work? Can we pull off a major shifting of the gears of the social order to provide human beings with a more balanced life and still have a healthy, productive economy? Do we have that now? Would it be a terrible risk to try a different way?

Research and Resource Information

Attitudes and Motivation

A large and continually growing body of formal social science research supports the key points made in this book. Fortunately, it is not always necessary to go to the original research reports, since much of the relevant work has been summarized in one of the following:

Daniel Yankelovich, *New Rules: Searching for Self-Fulfillment in a World Turned Upside Down.* New York: Random House, 1981. Summarizes large-scale research over 20 years to document the scope of changed attitudes toward work as well as toward other aspects of people's lives.

Clark Kerr and Jerome M. Rosow (eds.), *Work in America: The Decade Ahead.* New York: Van Nostrand Reinhold, 1979. A collection of analytical essays sponsored by the Work in America Institute, which includes Yankelovich's "Work, Values, and the New Breed" and Raymond A. Katzell's "Changing Attitudes Toward Work."

Mihaly Csikszentmihalyi, *Beyond Boredom and Anxiety.* San Francisco: Jossey-Bass, 1975. A summary of the author's own research, which clearly illuminates the importance of *intrinsic* motivation—the desire to engage in an activity because of internal urges rather than external rewards such as money or prestige.

Fred Best, *Exchanging Earnings for Leisure: Findings of an Exploratory National Survey on Work Time Preferences.* Washington, D.C., U.S. Department of Labor, 1980. Documents clearly the fact that many people, if given a choice, will trade income for free time.

Tibor Scitovsky, *The Joyless Economy: An Inquiry into Human Satisfaction and Dissatisfaction.* New York: Oxford University Press, 1976. Includes a concise summary of some of the major research by experimental psychologists on human motivation. A fascinating book by one of the world's great economists, who argues that the typical assumptions made by economists about human motivation are incorrect and therefore so is much of current economic theory.

Effects of Flexible Work Options on Productivity, Morale, and Other Variables

United States Senate Committee on Governmental Affairs, *Flexitime and Part-Time Legislation* (Report of Hearing, June 29, 1978). Testimony and related documents from a wide range of experts on flextime and part-time work arrangements. Data led to experimental implementation of these options in several departments of the federal government.

Stanley D. Nollen and Virginia H. Martin, *Alternative Work Schedules,* AMA Survey Reports, Part 1: *Flexitime;* Parts 2 and 3: *Permanent Part-Time Employment and the Compressed Workweek.* New York: AMACOM, 1978.

One of the largest projects involving job sharing is the state of Wisconsin's Project Join. A series of reports on this experience is available from the Bureau of Human Resource Services, Department of Administration, State of Wisconsin, Madison, Wisconsin.

Managing Time

Making the best use of work time so you can relax and enjoy free time is one of the major challenges of "working free." These books provide some valuable suggestions:

Alan Lakein, *How to Get Control of Your Time and Your Life.* New York: New American Library, 1973.

Dru Scott, Ph.D., *How to Put More Time in Your Life,* New York: Signet, 1980.

Alec Mackenzie and Kay Cronkite Waldo, *About Time! A Woman's Guide to Time Management.* New York: McGraw-Hill, 1981.

Money

Most of us, from time to time, have had the feeling that money, or the need of it, or the love of it, was running our lives. It is possible to get some perspective on the issue of money by taking a hard look at your own assumptions and conditioning on the subject. These books offer three very different perspectives on the money issue and will help you see more clearly how important or unimportant money is to you.

Michael Phillips, *The Seven Laws of Money.* New York: Random House, 1974.

Philip Slater, *Wealth Addiction* ("America's most powerful drug. How it weakens us. How we can free ourselves."). New York: Dutton, 1980.

Jerry Gillies, *Moneylove: How to Get the Money You Deserve for Whatever You Want.* New York: M. Evans & Co., 1978.

"Getting By on a Writer's Income," an article by Lawrence Block in *Writer's Digest,* October 1981, offers sage advice for a free-lancer in any trade.

An excellent book on increasing "quality of life" while living on less income is Duane Elgin's *Voluntary Simplicity,* New York: Morrow, 1981.

Work and the Rest of Your Life

This is a vast subject. How can people achieve some reasonable integration of work, leisure, learning, families, friends, intimate relationships, household management, volunteer work, artistic pursuits, and all the other things people like to do with their time and energy? Here are just a few of the author's favorite books that offer some useful perspectives:

E. F. Schumacher, with Peter Gillingham, *Good Work.* New York: Harper & Row, 1979.

Richard N. Bolles, *The Three Boxes of Life, and How to Get Out of Them.* Berkeley, Calif.: Ten Speed Press, 1978.

Sebastian deGrazia, *Of Time, Work, and Leisure.* New York: Twentieth Century Fund, 1962.

Staffan Linder, *The Harried Leisure Class.* New York: Columbia University Press, 1970.

Alvin Toffler, *The Third Wave.* New York: Morrow, 1980.

Sara Ruddick and Pamela Daniels (eds.), *Working It Out,* "23 Women Writers, Artists, Scientists, and Scholars Talk about Their Lives and Their Work." New York: Pantheon Books, 1977.

Jay B. Rohrlich, M.D., *Work and Love: The Crucial Balance.* New York: Summit Books, 1980.

On work and learning:

Ivar Berg, *Education and Jobs: The Great Training Robbery.* Boston: Beacon, 1971.

James O'Toole, *Work, Learning, and the American Future.* San Francisco: Jossey-Bass, 1977.

On work and family life:

Rosabeth Moss Kanter, *Work and Family in the United States.* New York: Russell Sage Foundation, 1977.

Kenneth Keniston and the Carnegie Council on Children, *All Our Children: The American Family Under Pressure.* New York: Harcourt Brace Jovanovich, 1977.

Caroline Bird, *The Two Paycheck Marriage: How Women at Work Are Changing Life in America.* New York: Rawson, Wade, 1979.

Finally, if a reader wishes to get a good picture of the possibilities for other dimensions of life when work is not the total controlling factor, spend a few evenings browsing through:

The Next Whole Earth Catalog. New York: Random House, 1981.

Getting Your Act Together

Most books dealing with personal-life assessment and clarification of personal values and goals present their messages on the assumption that the reader is looking for a traditional career or job. Nonetheless, many of these books contain useful exercises and ideas for people who may prefer to work on their own terms. You'll find some helpful ideas in:

Sidney B. Simon, Leland W. Howe, and Howard Kirschenbaum, *Values Clarification: A Handbook of Practical Strategies for Teachers and Students* [equally relevant for others]. New York: Hart, 1972.

Richard Nelson Bolles, *What Color Is Your Parachute? A Practical Manual for Job-Hunters and Career-Changers* (1975, occasionally revised); *The Three Boxes of Life, And How to Get Out of Them: An Introduction to Life/Work Planning* (1978); and John C. Crystal, *Where Do I Go from Here with My Life?* (1974). All three are published by Ten Speed Press, Berkeley, Calif.

Gordon Porter Miller, *Life Choices: How to Make the Critical Decisions—About Your Education, Career, Marriage, Family, Life Style.* New York: Crowell, 1978.

A nice concise booklet of simple exercises is Leland Howe's *Taking Charge of Your Life,* Niles, Ill.: Argus Communications, 1977.

All the writers mentioned offer workshops from time to time in major cities and some smaller towns. You can find out about them by writing the authors in care of their publishers.

We can learn a lot from other people's experiences, as I hope you have discovered in this book. And it's as useful to learn about some attempts to achieve freedom that didn't work out so well (why not learn from others' mistakes instead of having to make them all yourself?) as to learn from the success stories. Some good information along these lines is to be found in Bernard Lefkowitz's *Breaktime: Living Without Work in a Nine to Five World* (New York, Hawthorn, 1979) and *Radical Career Change: Life Beyond Work,* by David L. Krantz (New York, Free Press, 1978). These case studies make it quite clear that "freedom," by itself, isn't enough. On the more positive, constructive side, you may get some real inspiration from the first-person accounts in Raymond Mungo's *Cosmic Profit: How to Make Money Without Doing Time* (Boston: Atlantic/Little, Brown, 1979), Geof Hewitt's

Working for Yourself (Emmaus, Pa.: Rodale Press, 1977) and William C. Ronco's *Jobs: How People Create Their Own* (Boston: Beacon Press, 1977).

Jay Levinson, who earns money many different ways without ever working full-time, offers some good advice and a large number of specific ways to earn money in his *Earning Money Without a Job* (1976) and *555 Ways to Earn Extra Money* (1982). Both are published by Holt, Rinehart & Winston.

You can find some good information on the nuts and bolts of getting started on your own in *YOU, Inc.: A Detailed Escape Route to Being Your Own Boss,* by Peter Weaver (New York: Doubleday/Dolphin, 1973). If what you have in mind is a very small, perhaps home-based, business, you might want to browse through *The Mother Earth News Handbook of Home Business Ideas and Plans* (New York: Bantam Books, 1976). And if you think you always have to be competitive to succeed, your eyes will be opened by the stories of very small businesses cooperating and sharing resources in *The Briarpatch Book* (San Francisco: New Glide, 1978; these people also put out a regular newsletter), and Michael Phillips's *Honest Business* (New York: Random House, 1981).

Finally, if you want to earn your living as a potter, leatherworker, woodcrafter, photographer, or any other marketable craft, be sure to read Elyse Sommer's *Career Opportunities in Crafts,* "with more than 55 success stories" (New York: Crown, 1977).

Support Systems and Networks

If your chosen path is anything even remotely resembling a small business venture (I include such things as free-lance writing or photography, counseling, independent teaching, and other similar occupations), you will have to manage money in an organized way. This is one area where it will pay to be very *conventional.* There is good help:

Bernard Kamoroff, C.P.A., *Small-Time Operator,* "How to Start Your Own Small Business, Keep Your Books, Pay Your Taxes, and Stay Out of Trouble." The best beginners' guide to the nitty-gritty there is, including all the ledgers and worksheets you will need for a year. If your bookstore doesn't have it, order from Bell Springs Pub. Co., P.O. Box 322, Laytonville, Calif. 95454.

For those of you working at home, there's the National Alliance of Homebased Businesswomen, a membership organization that has published a useful book, *Women Working at Home: The Homebased Business Guide and Directory* (P.O. Box 95, Norwood, N.J. 07648. An excellent newsletter called "Mind Your Own Business at Home" (six issues per year $18) is available from Coralee Kern, 2520 North Lincoln Ave., P.O. Box 60, Chicago, Ill. 60614.

There is also a splendid bimonthly magazine for people involved in very small businesses that is always chock full of good information on how others are doing it and good advice from various specialists. Reading it from cover to cover will keep your courage up and probably improve your efficiency and enjoyment of your work:

In Business, Box 323, Emmaus, Pa. 18049 (six issues $13.97).

Three organizations have been working very effectively for many years to educate employers and individuals in the benefits and possibilities that come with new, more flexible ways of arranging work:

Catalyst, 14 East 60th Street, New York, N.Y. 10022.

New Ways to Work, 149 Ninth Street, San Francisco, Calif. 94103.

National Council for Alternative Work Patterns, 1925 K Street N.W., Suite 308A, Washington, D. C. 20006.

Each of these is a good source of up-to-date information. Catalyst has a fine resource library on the premises which is open to the public.

Here are some other resource, information, and consulting groups around the United States:

The Human Economy Center, P.O. Box 551, Amherst, Mass. 01004. The group is concerned with improvement of the quality of life through alternatives to conventional work arrangements.

Help available includes a quarterly newsletter, a comprehensive bibliography, and workshops, seminars, and consultation services.

Workshare, 311 East 50th Street, New York, N.Y. 10022. Patricia Lee, interviewed in this book, is director. Workshare has a membership network and a highly informative quarterly newsletter, and it offers frequent workshops.

Flexible Careers, 37 South Wabash, Chicago, Ill. 60603.

Focus, 509 Tenth Avenue East, Seattle, Wash. 98102.

Women's Center of Dallas, 2800 Routh Street, #197, Dallas, Texas 75201.

Work Time Alternatives, P.O. Box 7514, Albuquerque, N.M. 87194.

Job Sharers, Inc., P.O. Box 1542, Arlington, Va. 22210.

Flexible Ways to Work, c/o YWCA, 1111 S.W. Tenth Street, Portland, Ore. 97205.

Flexible Careers Project, P.O. Box 6701, Santa Barbara, Calif. 93111.

Work Options for Women, 321 Market St., Wichita, Kan. 67202.

Women's Work Project, 1 Harris Street, Newburyport, Mass. 01950.

CHART, 123 East Grant Street, Suite 1210, Minneapolis, Minn. 55403.

YWCAs in many locations offer resources, workshops, and information on flexible work options.

A special note to men: Much of the important trailblazing in this field has been done by and for women. But men should not be hesitant about seeking information and help from women's organizations. They're usually glad to help anyone who is interested—and wouldn't be caught dead discriminating against anyone on the basis of sex!

We've used the term "networking" a lot in this book. If you want to know more about how it's done and get some information about specific groups, consult the book *Networking—The First Report and Directory,* by Jessica Lipnack and Jeffrey Stamps, New York: Doubleday, 1982.

Free-lancers of every sort may want to check out Support Services Alliance, Inc., Two Times Square, New York, N.Y. 10036. Tel: (212) 398-7800. This not-for-profit group is set up to provide free-lancers and very small businesses such things as group insurance, discounts on copying machines and rental cars, and similar services. They also offer a newsletter and occasional workshops and seminars.

Inventors and others with good ideas for new businesses might find a hospitable home for a while at Rensselaer Polytechnic Institute, Troy, New York. This prestigious engineering school has recently begun offering office and work space for next to nothing, and access to other Institute facilities including the Business School faculty.

For people who want to travel, see the world, and still earn some money, there are a surprising number of opportunities. An excellent introduction to this whole area is:

Max Steele, *Seasonal Jobs on Land and Sea,* New York, Harper Colophon, 1979. Includes many lists of specific places you may find various kinds of temporary work.

The indispensible handbook for the world traveler is:

The Directory of Overseas Summer Jobs, published annually by Vacation-Work, 9 Park End Street, Oxford, England. Distributed in the United States by Writer's Digest Books, 9933 Alliance Road, Cincinnati, Ohio 45242; in Canada: Henry Fletcher Services, Ltd., 304 Taylor Road, West Hill, Ontario, M1C 2R6.

There is also an excellent magazine covering both work and learning opportunities abroad:

Transitions ($5 a year for 4 issues), 18 Hulst Road, Amherst, Mass. 01002.

If you just want to see the U. S. A., you'll want to get:

Summer Employment Directory of the United States. It is published annually by Writer's Digest Books in Cincinnati.

Writer's Digest is an excellent monthly magazine for free-lance writers. It includes many good tips and lots of useful information, much of which is just as relevant to other kinds of free-lancing—for example, a recent article on "How to Live on a Writer's Income." They also publish the handbooks *Writer's Mar-*

ket and *Photographer's Market,* which tell you how and where to sell your work.

Some high-powered help is available to anyone starting or managing a small business through the Service Corps of Retired Executives, 26 Federal Plaza, New York, N.Y. 10278. This group has chapters all over the United States, and services are offered free of charge. The New York City group typically counsels up to 10,000 people each year. Whether or not you live near an affiliated group, you'll find that retired people are usually glad to share their knowledge and experience as long as they don't get the feeling you are wasting their time.

I will be offering workshops on "Working Free" and "Inventing Your Own Job" from time to time in various U.S. and Canadian locations. For further information on these workshops write John Applegath, c/o The Human Economy Center, P.O. Box 551, Amherst, Mass. 01004.

Finally, we expect that this book will prove useful enough so that there will be subsequent printings and revised editions. I would like to have information about other support systems and networks not mentioned here for inclusion in future editions. And, of course, any other suggestions or good information you might care to share is welcome.

Enlightened Employers—Flexible Work Arrangements in Traditional Work Settings

These books provide detailed information on several variations of nonconventional work scheduling, including a number of case studies and evaluation research:

Simcha Ronen, Ph.D., *Flexible Working Hours.* New York: McGraw-Hill, 1981. The most up-to-date reference in the field of alternative work schedules.

Maureen E. McCarthy and Gail S. Rosenberg, *Work Sharing Case Studies,* Kalamazoo, Mich.: The W. E. Upjohn Institute for Employment Research, 1981. The best source for detailed case study analyses.

J. Carroll Swart, *A Flexible Approach to Working Hours.* New York: AMACOM, 1978. A thorough analysis of several versions of flextime.

Douglas L. Fleuter, *The Workweek Revolution.* Reading, Mass.: Addison-Wesley, 1975. A brief overview of flextime and shortened work weeks.

Archibald A. Evans, *Flexibility in Working Life: Opportunities for Individual Choice.* Paris: Organization for Economic Cooperation and Development, 1973. Good overview of the European experience with unconventional work arrangements.

Gretl S. Meier, *Job Sharing: A New Pattern for Quality of Work and Life.* Kalamazoo, Mich.: The W. E. Upjohn Institute for Employment Research, 1979. A highly informative analysis of the most interesting new development in enlightened work arrangements. Includes material drawn from interviews with 84 job sharers and an excellent list of further readings.

For a good list of employers who have implemented flextime, shorter work weeks, permanent part-time jobs, and job sharing, see:

Alternative Work Schedule Director. Washington, D.C.: National Council for Alternative Work Patterns, 1979.

Index

accountant, need for, 150
Agee, William, 161
All Our Children—The American Family Under Pressure (Keniston), 114
artists, and intrinsic motivation, 47
assembly-lines, workers in, 5–6
Authority (Sennett), 139

Baer, Suzanne, 2
Barley, Betsy, 35–37, 53–54, 58–59, 100–101, 154
bartering, as substitute for income, 143–144, 159
Berg, Ivar, 105
Best, Fred, 42–43
Beyond Boredom and Anxiety (Csikszentmihalyi), 178
biological clocks, and work routines, 13, 33, 95
Bird, Caroline, *ix–xi*, 40
Bohen, Halcy, 113–114
Bolle, Richard, 141
Burns, Wendy, 2–3

California, University of, at Los Angeles, 110
Callaway, John, 108–109, 111

Canadians, in statistics, 9–10
"Catalyst," 114
Center for Advanced Study in the Behavioral Sciences, 89
chef, as flexible career option, 20
child-care, and work arrangements, 113–114
Clebus, Joan, 95–96
clocks, biological, and work routines, 13, 33, 95
computer conferencing, 156
computer programming, as flexible career option, 6, 20
consulting, as flexible work option, 20
Continental Illinois National Bank & Trust Company, 163
continuing education, 14, 104, 110–112, 184–186
Control Data Corporation, 163
Cosenza, Joan Likely, 2
Cosmic Profit: How to Earn Money Without Doing Time (Mungo), 89
cottage, electronic, as work model, 6, 19, 119
cottage industries, 118–119
Courage to Create, The (May), 141
Crystal, John, 141

Csikszentmihalyi, Mihaly, 178

Dagdigian, Ken, 91
Dickson, Paul, 165
Directory of the National Council for Alternative Work Patterns, 168
dissatisfaction with traditional jobs, reasons for, 23
Donne, John, 151

Earning Money Without a Job (Levinson), 125
Edison, Thomas, 20
education, continuing, 14, 104, 110–112, 184–186
education, formal
  myth of, 104–111, 136
  need for, 102–103, 105
  restructuring of, 185–186
Edwards, Patsy, 104–105
efficiency, and redistribution of work, 180–181
Eitzenhoefer, Stephan, 111–112, 127–128, 129
elderly, and work redistribution, 189–190
"electronic cottage," as work model, 6, 19, 119
employers, enlightened, 162–170, 179–180
entertainment industry
  free-lancers and, 182
  time management and, 91–94
  union benefits and, 160
equipment, acquiring, 148
Europe, enlightened employment in, 163

factories, as models for institutions, 6
Federman, Andy, 57–58, 59, 60, 83–85, 93–94, 96, 160

Fiske, Donald, 13
555 Ways to Earn Extra Money (Levinson), 125
flexible work options, for employers, 162–170, 179–180
flextime, 15–16
Forbes and Wagner, 165–166
Ford Foundation, 10–11, 163
free-lancing, as flexible work option, 18–19
Future of the Workplace, The (Dickson), 165

Galbraith, Jane, 1, 128–129
Galbraith, John Kenneth, 1
Galbraith, Mike, 1, 94, 112, 128–129
Gardiner, Scot, 19, 122–123, 149
Gillingham, Peter, 171
Goldstein, Jerome, 113
Good Work (Schumacher and Gillingham), 171
Grace, Mary, 21
Graves, Robin, 2–3
Grinberg, Miguel, 53

Harris, Louis, survey by, 43
Hassan, Michael, 37–38, 123
Heath, Willis, 110
Henkel, Ludwig, 39
Hewlett-Packard, 163
home, as workplace, 19–20, 117–125
How to Get Control of Your Time and Your Life (Lakein), 149
Human Economy Center, 157, 183
Hutchins, Robert, 110

income
  downward adjustment of, 56
  minimum levels of, 72–87

information economy, 118–119
Ingle, Grant, 58
Institute for Liberty and Community, 118

Jacobs, Dorri, 60–61, 136, 155
Japan, management in, 43
job security, desire for, 43
job sharing, 2, 17–18, 21
Job Sharing: A New Pattern for Quality of Work and Life (Meier), 18
Joyless Economy, The (Scitovsky), 26

Kanter, Rosabeth Moss, 114
Kaplan, Felicia, 50–51, 62, 63–64, 76–78, 115, 155–156, 157, 158
Keck, Barbara, 39, 113
Keynes, John Maynard, 20

Labor Department (U.S.), 10
Labor Ministry of Canada, 10
Lakein, Alan, 149
Lao-tsu, 50, 135
Learning Exchange (Evanston, Ill.), 110, 156
Lee, Pat, 2, 3, 28–30, 55, 63, 70, 76, 112, 115, 117, 120–121, 132, 137, 146, 158
leisure, desire for, 42–43
Levinson, Jay, 2, 3, 14, 21, 67, 77, 115, 122, 125, 129–130, 158–159
Liewbow, Elliot, 22
life-experience, and nontraditional work possibilities, 137–139
Lipnack, Jessica, 97–98, 121–123, 129, 130, 133, 158
Livingston, Dennis, 156
Living Well Is the Best Revenge

(Tompkins), 152
Love, Sam, 2, 66, 74, 75, 90–91

Machlowitz, Marian, 8
Man in the Gray Flannel Suit, The (Wilson), 45
Marien, Mike, 2, 115, 119–120
Marriott, Bob, 31–33, 54, 58, 66, 74, 82–83, 91, 120, 129, 130, 136–137
Marriott, Jane, 31–33, 54, 66, 74, 82–83, 120, 121, 129, 130
Maslow, Abraham, 63
May, Ernest, 106–107
May, Rollo, 63, 141
McCarthy, Maureen, 166
McClaughry, John, 118
Meier, Gretl S., 18
Metzger, Don, 2, 3, 62, 69–70, 94–95, 96, 115
Michael, Donald, 54, 98–99
Miller, Judith, 28
Miller, William, 107
Mitts, Charles, 159
Moffat, Sebastian, 49–50, 131
Mollner, Terry, 1, 3, 33–34, 54, 70–71, 97, 112, 115, 136
money, assessing need for, 142–147
Monnet, Jean, 52
Moss, Roy, 167
mothers, and work arrangements, 113–114
motivation, workers
  extrinsic, 43–46
  intrinsic, 44–51, 63, 90
Mungo, Raymond, 89

National Commission for Manpower Policy, 42–43
National Council for Alternative Work Patterns, 114, 162, 168

networks, 151–160
"New Breed," and traditional
values, 42, 52, 56
New School (New York City), 110
"Newsletter of the National
Council for Alternative Work
Patterns," 166
"New Ways to Work" (Califor-
nia), 114, 169

O'Brien, Darcy, 107
Organization Man, The (Whyte), 45
"Outward Bound," 50, 55, 140

part-time work, 16–17
Pavilon, Mike, 50–51, 83, 140
Peacock, Ted, 167–168
Peitz, John, 127
Phillips, Michael, 87, 144
Picasso, Pablo, 20
Pickering, Alan, 72–73
Plan for the Rational Distribution
of Work, 174–177
"Playboy Report on the American
Male," 43–44
"Pleasures and Pitfalls of a Busi-
ness at Home, The," (Som-
mer), 124
productivity, and work routines,
13–21
"Project Join" (Wisconsin), 165
publishing, and decentralization,
182

Raney, Carol, 37
real estate, sale of, as flexible
career option, 20
retirement, planning for, 126–
134
rewards
intrinsic, 27, 44–51, 63–71
monetary, 24–25, 27, 42–43

risks, taking, 53–61, 127, 150,
183
Ritchie, Art, 35
Rizzo, Francine, 33, 85, 88, 127,
133
Rogers, Carl, 63
Rosenberg, Gail, 166
Rumble, Terry, 17

Sager, Norm, 165
Salk, Jonas, 109
Schneider, Peter, 186
Schrank, Robert, 10, 151
Schulze, Steve, 124–125
Schumacher, E. F., 171
Scitovsky, Tibor, 26
security, and the future, 127–
134, 144–145
self-assessment, and preparation
for nontraditional work,
137–147
self-discipline, and nontraditional
work routines, 89–90, 123–
124, 148–149
Sennett, Richard, 139, 145
Seven Laws of Money, The (Phillips), 87, 144
Shakespeare, William, 62
sharing, job, 2, 17–18, 21
Simon's Rock College (Massachusetts), 110
Slater, Philip, 72, 87, 144
socializing, in work productivity,
151–152
Society for Human Economy,
157, 183
Sommer, Elyse, 124, 125
Stamps, Jeffrey, 97–98, 129, 158
standard of living, adjustment of,
56, 73–87, 142–147
statistics, sources for, 10
Stryker, Jay, 118

Stuhrcke, Diane, 164
Sucher, Cobi, 46–49, 57–58, 62,
    65–66, 78–81, 91, 96–97,
    112, 115, 120, 126, 133–134
support systems, 151–160
Sylvester, Rowlie, 85–87, 115,
    135–136, 147–148, 166–167

Targ, William, 107–108, 111
taxes, and nontraditional work,
    144–145, 150
Ten Thousand Working Days
    (Schrank), 151–152
Terkel, Studs, 135–136, 137
Third Wave, (The Toffler), 19
Thurow, Lester, 171
time, management of, 88–101
Toffler, Alvin, 6, 19, 119
Trusteeship Institute, 34

U.C.L.A., extension college, 110
unemployment, and redistribu-
    tion of work, 187–188

values
    institutional, 46
    shift in, among workers, 41–45

Wachtel, Irma, 64–65, 67, 115,
    137, 156
Wakefield, Dick, 82, 158
Watts, Alan, 141
Wealth Addiction (Slater), 72, 87,
    144
Webb, Tom, 56–57
Weber, Max, 102

Werner, Douglas, 59, 68–69, 75,
    91–93, 155
What Color is Your Parachute?
    (Bolle), 141
*Where Do I Go From Here with My
    Life?* (Crystal), 141
Williams, Michele, 60, 74–75,
    123, 155–156, 157–158, 164
Wilson, Beverly, 181
Wisdom of Insecurity, The (Watts),
    141
word-processing systems, 6
work
    identity and, 102–103
    institutional viewpoint of, 43–
    45
    military model of, 3
    redistribution of, 172–177,
    180–181, 187
Work and Family in the United States
    (Kanter), 114
work ethic, 14, 126
workforce, impressions of, 4–6
Work in America: The Decade Ahead
    (Yankelovich), 41–42
workshops, for work and life
    planning, 141
World Future Society, The, 2, 11
Writer's Digest, 154
Writer's Market, 154

Yankelovich, Daniel, 41–42, 52
Yankelovich, Skelly & White, 41

Zero-Sum Society, The (Thurow),
    171

AMACOM Executive Books—Paperbacks

John Applegath	Working Free	$6.95
John D. Arnold	The Art of Decision Making: 7 Steps to Achieving More Effective Results	$6.95
Alec Benn	The 27 Most Common Mistakes in Advertising	$5.95
Dudley Bennett	TA and the Manager	$6.95
Don Berliner	Want a Job? Get Some Experience ...	$5.95
Blake & Mouton	Productivity—The Human Side	$5.95
Borst & Montana	Managing Nonprofit Organizations	$6.95
George A. Brakeley	Tested Ways to Successful Fund Raising	$8.95
Ronald D. Brown	From Selling to Managing	$5.95
Richard E. Byrd	A Guide to Personal Risk Taking	$5.95
Logan Cheek	Zero-Base Budgeting Comes of Age	$6.95
William A. Cohen	The Executive's Guide to Finding a Superior Job	$5.95
Ken Cooper	Bodybusiness	$5.95
James J. Cribbin	Effective Managerial Leadership	$6.95
William Dowling	Effective Management & the Behavioral Sciences	$8.95
Richard J. Dunsing	You and I Have Simply Got to Stop Meeting This Way	$5.95
Sidney Edlung	There Is a Better Way to Sell	$5.95
Elam & Paley	Marketing for the Nonmarketing Executive	$5.95
Norman L. Enger	Management Standards for Developing Information Systems	$6.95
John Fenton	The A to Z of Sales Management	$7.95
Figueroa & Winkler	A Business Information Guidebook	$9.95
Saul W. Gellerman	Motivation and Productivity	$6.95
Roger A. Golde	Muddling Through	$5.95
Hanan Berrian, Cribbin, & Donis	Success Strategies for the New Sales Manager	$8.95
Lois B. Hart	Moving Up! Women and Leadership	$6.95
Hart & Schleicher	A Conference and Workshop Planner's Manual	$15.95
Michael Hayes	Pay Yourself First	$6.95
Hilton & Knoblauch	On Television	$6.95
Herman R. Holtz	The $100 Billion Market	$10.95
Herman R. Holtz	Profit From Your Money-Making Ideas	$8.95
Charles L. Hughes	Goal Setting	$5.95
John W. Humble	How to Manage By Objectives	$5.95
Jones & Trentin	Budgeting (rev. ed.)	$12.95
Donald J. Kenney	Minicomputers	$7.95
William H. Krause	How to Get Started as a Manufacturers' Representative	$8.95
Sy Lazarus	Loud & Clear: A Guide to Effective Communication	$5.95

Wayne A. Lemmon	The Owner's and Manager's Market Analysis Workbook	$9.95
George J. Lumsden	Impact Management	$6.95
Philip R. Lund	Compelling Selling	$5.95
Charles Margerison	Assessing Your Managerial Style	$6.95
Dale D. McConkey	No-Nonsense Delegation	$5.95
Robert J. McKain, Jr.	Realize Your Potential	$5.95
Edward S. McKay	The Marketing Mystique	$6.95
Donald E. Miller	The Meaningful Interpretation of Financial Statements	$6.95
Robert L. Montgomery	Memory Made Easy	$5.95
Terry A. Mort	Systematic Selling	$6.95
William R. Osgood	Basics of Successful Business Planning	$7.95
Alfred R. Oxenfeldt	Pricing Strategies	$10.95
Oxenfeldt, Miller & Dickinson	A Basic Approach to Executive Decision Making	$7.95
Dean B. Peskin	A Job Loss Survival Manual	$5.95
Andrew Pleninger	How to Survive and Market Yourself in Management	$6.95
Edward N. Rausch	Financial Management for Small Business	$7.95
L. Gayle Rayburn	Financial Tools for Marketing Administration	$10.95
Elton T. Reeves	So You Want to Be a Supervisor (rev. ed.)	$6.95
Rinella & Robbins	Career Power	$7.95
Paula I. Robbins	Successful Midlife Career Change	$7.95
Edward Roseman	Confronting Nonpromotability	$5.95
William E. Rothschild	Putting It All Together	$7.95
H. Lee Rust	Jobsearch	$7.95
Hank Seiden	Advertising Pure and Simple	$5.95
Robert Seidenberg	Corporate Wives . . . Corporate Casualties?	$6.95
Roger W. Seng	The Skills of Selling	$7.95
Andrew H. Souerwine	Career Strategies	$7.95
Summer & Levy, eds.	Microcomputers for Business	$7.95
Curtis W. Symonds	Basic Financial Management (rev. ed.)	$5.95
William C. Waddell	Overcoming Murphy's Law	$5.95
Murray L. Weidenbaum	The Future of Business Regulation	$5.95
Allen Weiss	Write What You Mean	$5.95
Leon A. Wortman	A Deskbook of Business Management Terms	$14.95
Leon A. Wortman	Successful Small Business Management	$5.95
Wortman & Sperling	Defining the Manager's Job (rev. ed.)	$9.95
Jere E. Yates	Managing Stress	$5.95